THE MAKING

A Young American's Search for Riches in the Land Down Under

Dear Dr. Holly,

You are such an Awesome Soul. Thank you so much for Helping so many.

You are an inspiration to many.

I hope you enjoy my story. + Prosper in 2014.

THE MAKING

A Young American's Search for Riches in the Land Down Under

The Making
A Young American's Search for Riches in the Land
Down Under

Copyright © 2013 Dominic Kotarski

Published by Sarcio Solutions
1-888-632-7443

Interior Design and Cover Design by Summer Bay Press
Editing by Summer Bay Press

ISBN: 978-0-9936122-1-3
Digital ISBN: 978-0-9936122-0-6

TESTIMONIALS

Dominic Kotarski's book was simultaneously engaging, insightful and witty. I read it in one sitting and came away feeling that anything was possible if you set your mind to it no matter who you are or what type of experiences you've had. His intertwining of life events and sales acumen as well as great tips for personal development, will make your mood euphoric long after you finish your read.
Colin Gerrard, CEO of EWS CONSULTING and 7 COLLI PRODUCTIONS

"The Making" is an impressive and very personal account of Kotarski's lifelong quest into how to build a successful career in sales. It helps you to understand what is needed to realize a successful sale and how to build discipline into your daily work routine. This book is a must read for every entrepreneur and actually everybody in business.
Camiel Gielkens, General Manager, Schouten China

"The Making" By Dominic Kotarski, is a Fantastic Book! Very easy to read, and digest, with invaluable content, for both "Newbies" to Sales, and "Seasoned Professionals". If you are Serious, and Sincere about continuing to develop your Sales, Business, Management, and People Skills, "The Making" is an essential read for yourself, and indeed for "Your Team"!!
Richard Fox, Sales Director, EMEA, GoGrid.com

Although it's a no brainer that this book "The Making" should be included as standard equipment for everyone who is involved in sales. I would also highly recommend it for everybody who is interested in getting more insight and understanding into the psychology behind the art of persuasion and selling. Dominic shows how a good mix of ambition, self-criticism, eagerness to learn, and for sure, a lot of fun paved his way to success. The book is about sales but in a broader sense it is the story of a young man who is making his dream come true.
Coco Geluk, Managing Director Landis+Gyr Netherlands

I got into sales when I was a young 22-year-old fresh off the construction sites as a bricklayer. I went through the same recruiting and training process as Dominic highlights in "The Making." He covers all the points that are required to become a super-successful person in the field of business, all you have to do is; know it, understand it and follow it. I am so glad I got to meet Dominic at a point in my life when I needed guidance and leadership the most. I will say that a lot of my success is down to him making me believe in myself at a point when I was about to turn around and quit. He made me believe in a system at a time when I was thinking success is about luck; and I ain't a lucky person. Following his system has worked for me and I'm positive it will for you too.
Harvey Pogrund, CEO Hannah Direct

When you find and believe in an opportunity, your success or failure will be determined by the boundaries you set. Great work habits, ethics, passion and honesty are traits common in all successful people. Dominic's story will show you how to develop these qualities, as well as, how to maintain a forever-ongoing student mentality so you too can open doors in your own successful business journey. I highly recommend this book to those who seek true knowledge on how to build these solid foundations in order to create a secure and successful future.

Stephen Adgemis, Managing Director Appco Group Hellas S.A.

Dominic Kotarski is without doubt one of the most inspiring people I know. He combines excellent management skills on both an operational and strategic level. "The Making" describes the beginning of Dominic's journey that made him become the powerful leader and great communicator he is today. He will inspire you to develop your ability to get people motivated and get things happening in your business. Dominic has changed people's lives for the better, all over the world – especially mine. Thanks for this, Dom, and for sharing your knowledge and wisdom in "The Making".

Troy Mobbs, Founder & President of Cobra Group Indonesia.

"I have known Dominic for over 20 years and he never ceases to amaze me with his thirst for knowledge in order to succeed. He also has a great willingness to pass on that knowledge to teach people how to succeed in life & business. "The Making" is a complete sharing of this profitable information. Not only is he a great mentor, he has become a great friend as well. I had the privilege of joining his coaching company in 2005, and being able to watch him on a daily basis has led to my success in coaching as well. Thank you Dominic, I know "The Making" will improve the lives of Sales Professionals around the World.

Billy McIntosh, Sales Trainer/Coach & Author

"Dominic and I have worked closely together on and off since 1989. He has always shown a passion, patience, and skill for teaching. Not only was this book entertaining but also the sales lessons and insights he is presenting are tried, tested, and essential for anyone looking for a unique edge in their sales and sales management careers. "The Making" is a must read."
Douglas S. Thompson, Sales/Marketing Consultant & Entrepreneur

Acknowledgements

First and foremost I would like to thank my wife, Christina Waschko, for sharing her insight into how to get my thoughts out of my head and heart and into this book. Without her support and guidance along the way this project might still be stuck somewhere inside me.

I want to thank all the people I've been blessed to work with over the years. You've all touched me, inspired me, frustrated me, helped me, motivated me, taught me and shared so much with me over the years. Thanks for being who you are and staying true to your life's goals. In no particular order, Chris Niarchos, Steve Adgemis, Debbie Illife, Sue Oliver, Jeff Ponech, Colin Gerrard, Harvey Pogrund, Troy Mobbs, Dave Green, Mike Blane, Taras Koochin, Dim Adgemis, Marcus Foot, Patrick Monrad, Stewart Hartley, Shane Ward, Dave Burton, Emilie Nelson, Tony Fernandez, Nick Caley, Debbie Shaw, Eric Fustier, Doug Thompson, Michael Scully, Steve Nugent, Danny Mugarura, Ossie Smith, Billy McIntosh, Alan Wood, Melissa Ryan, Perveen Virdee, Michelle Green, Ali Pye, Richard Fox, Steve Dolan, Kelly Maclachlan, Peter Hancock, Peter Faddy, Jimmy Dancja, Mike Gittens, Byron Christie, Romano Imerini, Marc & Saddie Scott, Maechi Ebo, Paul Bender, Hamish Allen, Tony Ashby, Richard Davison, Avie Roth, Trish Dardis, Dave Fishman, Michelle Goodwin, Tim Hart, Karl Hensen, Alan Mehmet, Kate Webb, Lorna Ryan, Chaz Mehmet, Murray Reinhart, Darren Furlotte, Roy Goderie, Gianna Regonini, Chris Illiffe, Jeff Lewis, John

Keller, Tony Martino, Simon Wright, Daryll McGuire, Tom Phelan, Dionna Simich, Mick Sweeney, Tony Purcell, Johnny Robinson, Lee Wildman, Despina Yianokas, Deborah Jobben, Tony Carter, Said Ayatollahy,, Dennis Griffith, Gio DeGreef, Jez Davies, James Foster, Nancy Johnston, Nancy Hyde, Nevena Lukic, Emile Heeneman, Roderick Habermehl, Camiel Gilekens, Len Steele, Huib Zevenhuizen, Sjuul van der leeuw, Richard Spiler, Hamid Acharrab, Jeff Sawari, Dirk-Jan Rol, Daan Heeneman, Richard Blane, Ron Schotman, Gert-Jan Hoefman, Coco Geluk, Pim Breukelman, Chander Baktawar,, Douwe Baarsma, Roel Piergoelam, Camiel Gilekens, Greg Enser, Dennis Simmich, Youri Kuper, Nicholas Horsley, Michael Pahladsingh, Riny Kuyper, Andrew McRae, Jeroen Steenbakkers, Henk Smit, Peter Jan Keuning, Karen Kurtenbach, Julie Renyard, Boaz Jansens, Anne-Meint Bouma, Elton Westmas, John de Jong, Sanjeev Sampat, Stefan Quest, Mark Lieftink, Steven Abdoelhafiezkhan, Romy ter Haak, Redouan Furrer, Tammo Murris, John Adgemis, Gordon Michis, Wilco van der Jagt, Colin Phillips, Jadim Philips, Jiska Rodenburg, Reza Badoella, David Boven, Peter Klinge, Izabella Szachniewicz, Jochum Jarigsma, Rosalie Dykhuizen, Tommy kallon, James Greaves, Henk Getrouw, Aaron Baskerville, Yudith Yeabsley, Mehmet Isik, Ken & Kathy Bauso, Manos Markakis, Martine du Bois, Larry Tenenbaum, Henri Kerkvliet, Ben Freeman, Dave Lagudi, Michelle Sengupta, Mo Fox, Neils Heeremans, Ellen Hendricks, Marcel van Oers, Nikki Fasolo, Petra Kramer, Sweeb, Paul Viliunas, Robert Prins, Ali Yavuz, Resa Nasiri, Eric Kugler, Sam Holt, Jim McCarthy, Neil Spivak, Rene van der Jagt, Leon Smart, Dave Burgess, Christina Sorensen, Kevin O'Byrne, Neil Jackson, Alan O'Donoghue, Steven Ghoerbien, Erna De Koning, Gary Lewis, Mark Cox, Mike Cosgrove, Ryan McLellan, Danielle Saldanha, Marc

Featherstone, Erik van Putten, Aad Leenders, Jossy Albertus, Olivier Blomme, Jos Kerkhof, Dax Krenn, Carlos Zhu, Arvin Lu, Eric Sat, Kidi Chen, Avril Blake, Emma Mumby, Joy Rajasooriar,Chris Mandaracas, Vince McKay, Debbie Papaioanou, Christina Yiannoullou, Saud Dastagir, Wirin Ramhit, Sander Woelders, Willemijn Severijnse-Rhee, Samira Noor Amatul, Steve Sapsford, Arash Aryan, Steve Allen, Matt Kitchiner, Noe Feikema-Sandong, Amir Ghavami, Tristan Rowe, Coleman York, Micheal Prestia, Ali Mir, Ali Miri, Milad Najjar, Jethro van Putten, Daniel Iglic, Bobby Graham, Saurahb Singh, Simon Murphy, Imi Rtist, Marlo Gemert, Arief Lautan, Matt Angus, Barbara ten Tije, Babak Adlkish, Bernadette Beck, Prins Jaspal, Natalie Miras, Steve Adams, Imane Rhajdane, Arie Kwakernaat, Chris Jensen, Carly Toekaja, Shelley Spencer, Dave de Wit, Sapana Raval, Finbarr Horgan, Joolz Foster, Les Adams, Sophie Lu, Willem Schutte, Wim Backhuys, Carol & Mike Cosgrove, Tara Casey, Satjay Sharma, Peter Driessen, Shahvir Pestonji, Tai Hussain, Chris Mandaracus, Boyd Zeekaf, Dennis Sardjoe, Ochanie Pas, Danielle Samson, Peter Daman, Lazslo Kugyuelka, Rinus Schaasberg, Jaap Boiler, Dik Kok, Brian Quinn, Gilles Baudet, Grant Thompson, John Lyotier, Jan Mendes, Kim Somers, Andre Kok, Kaiwen Jiang, Yao Zhang and Anne Bruinsma to name only a few. There are countless others whom I've had the honor of to work with over the years. Although, I've not been able to include everyone on this list let it be known that my life has been altered in a multitude of positive ways, subtle and otherwise, by working with these amazing people. You know who you are ☺

DEDICATION

My three sons - you inspire me in every way, every day.
My wife Christina - your esprit is our guiding light.
My parents – for your love and encouragement to "make
my own way."

INTRODUCTION

This book is one of those stories that just had to come out. All my life people have told me I needed to write a book about all my early sales experiences. My friends and parents thought I was insane to leave America and travel half way around the world to Australia to find my fortune. This story takes place in 1987, a time before either the Internet or mobile phones were ubiquitous. The stock markets around the world had just experienced a huge crash known as Black Monday. Most of my friends were embarking on their safe careers. We had all just graduated from college and were chasing our futures. My choice was to pursue the unknown, I was made fun of and ridiculed by so many people for choosing to leave my country and pursue my crazy dreams. All I could think at the time was how right it all felt. I yearned to take the leap and follow the unbeaten path. Now that I've had the chance to look back over my decision, I cherish the fact that I had the guts to go it alone and search for my treasure.

Little did I know at the time that by taking these first steps I was paving my own way to experience so much of the world. Through my sales and business career I've been able to live and work in eleven different countries around the world. In these pages I will share with you the business foundation and frameworks needed to create a business that will allow you to do the same. I've earned the freedom to take a brief sabbatical so I can chart, relay and relive my experiences through these pages.

In today's world of Internet billionaires, social media giants, millionaire app developers and viral video creators this book will take you back to timeless sales skills, persuasion tactics, negotiation techniques and out and out motivational speaking. These skills are readily needed in today's business world and have been slowly dropping off at a time when they're needed the most. My aim in sharing my story with you is to revive your skill set and your mind set by exposing you to business wisdom that will serve you throughout the rest of your sales and business career. Happy reading. ☺

My Fellow Entrepreneurs,

I know it's not easy. Nothing worthwhile ever is. I know you are struggling and wondering if you should just throw in the towel and quit. I know you wish it could just get easier or that you could just get passed this most recent issue. Well, I want you to know that struggles and challenges are what actually make you and build your character. I want you to know that you're not alone.

Every great idea or accomplishment is borne out of struggle. There is always a point of pain that seems so great that the easiest option just seems to throw in the towel. Well, that option is always there if you need it. But the only thing that separates people who accomplish their life's goals and personal dreams from those who don't, is the decision to push through the pain barrier and carry on when it seems like everything is falling apart.

Anyone who has accomplished something worthwhile will tell you, it is at this point, the quitting point, the darkest point, when they made the decision to carry on. They decided the cost of quitting was too great and the fun of the journey ahead whatever it might bring was too alluring for them to admit defeat and give up.

I encourage you to do the same; make the same decision. You can always go back to your old life if you have to. Nobody will ever fault you for trying and you will always have one helluva story to tell.

Life is about thinking big, dreaming big and following our heart's desires. Our imaginations aren't meant to torture us. They're meant to inspire us to go beyond our fears and worries. Our imagination is geared towards creative problem solving. All we have to do is put ourselves in situations where the higher brain is forced to kick in and help us solve the issue. Make sure you keep your sense of humor along the way. We humans have the innate ability to take the best plans in the world and somehow manage to screw them up.

Case in point, I was living in London back when the British and French governments decided to build a tunnel under the English Channel. The tunnel would stretch from Kent, UK to Calais in France.

Some of the most brilliant engineers and minds of the time created the plans. The plan was to start digging the tunnel simultaneously on each end and meet in the middle. Sounds pretty simple and straightforward, doesn't it? So you can imagine what happened.

About halfway through the project the developers realized that they were not on course to meet in the middle. If you've ever crossed the channel on this wonderful train you will notice roughly half way through your journey there's a nice swerve to the left and back to the right. This slight corrective detour was necessary to connect the two tunnels and get the train "back on track", so to speak.

I always used to joke that both the French and the Brits forgot that the drivers in each nation drive on the opposite sides of the street. My point is that even the smartest people in the world and the strongest teams can take a simple plan like starting on opposite sides of the channel with the plan to meet in the middle and yet somehow still manage to screw it up.

The important thing to remember is that they did accomplish their goal. The tunnel got built. Millions of people now benefit from the combined effort, persistence and determination of people who finished what they set out to do, regardless of imperfections and setbacks along the way.

You must do the same. I'm here to encourage you to keep going, to develop and then share the skills that you need in order to complete your journey to the top of your profession. My motivation is to ensure you're able to profit from all your hard work, as well as to encourage you to leverage your skills and connections, so you can build the life and business you deserve.

Anyone who puts their mind to it can achieve their goals. You can, too, as long as you don't quit and are willing to do the work necessary both on yourself and with your team in order to reach the top.

What is the top you might ask? Great question!

First, it's important to understand how vital it is to have audacious goals. Even more important, is you must know your intentions behind those goals. I will go into depth about this topic later in this book.

Second, you can't quit. You must be committed to the journey and all that it brings, for better or sometimes worse, when you set your course. If you are willing to stick at it and commit the hours it will take to master your craft, you'll end up moving onwards and upwards. Your professional skills will develop and new opportunities will appear.

The top means to go as high as your company plan allows. That's the top. If your current company doesn't have any plans after you reach the highest position available then you can ask the owners, directors or shareholders to share the pie. Failing this, you could look for other opportunities. If neither of those options seems available then you could stay in your current position while developing yourself further through coaching, seminars or management courses. This might lead you on one of the most fulfilling options known to the free world – the decision to start your own company.

I will cover all of these topics in this book and will share with you stories from my experiences in all of these areas. By sharing my background you can get a better idea of where I'm coming from when I inspire you to follow your highest calling. Listen to the voice in your head that yearns to be free and speaks directly to your heart. It's yelling, Be Bold; Be Brave; Be strong and go for it today!

Chapter One

MY STORY- Australia is Calling

I was born and raised in Chattanooga, Tennessee. I grew up in a middle-class family in a suburb called East Ridge. My mom was a teacher and my dad worked for himself as a manufacturer's representative. I lead a pretty normal childhood enjoying friends and playing sports. I never really got much career advice or direction from my parents or my teachers. I was only told that I had to go to university. So I did the best I could to pass tests and get good enough grades to get into university but I didn't have any clue what I wanted to study or "be" when I grew up.

I think this is pretty typical of most young people, unless you show some amazing talent in a certain area or your parents are super ambitious and hardwired to spend their lives "making" their children good at something. Some parents are determined to have their child become a doctor or a lawyer because they see that as the ticket for their child's success.

My parents loved their children (I have a younger brother and older sister) too much to force anything on us. Like most parents, they just wanted us to be happy and make our own decisions. My dad's big thing was that we should learn to be "independent". Boy did I get a shock when I realized what that loving statement really meant. I would have to pay my own way through university.

This is the point where my story of learning the principles of success really starts. I am 100% sure it's the same for you. It is that point when you know you are expected to do something but you really don't have any clue how you're going to do it. It is good that you are faced with this type of adversity when you are young because you will have the boldness of youth on your side. You know you also have time on your side and your imagination permits you to see a brighter future. You are moving forward in life, not just because you want to and are excited to gain new experiences, but also because you are expected to, by your parents, teachers, coaches and mentors.

As we grow older and our responsibilities increase we often lose the carefree boldness of youth. This doesn't mean that we should not keep challenging ourselves to learn new things as we get older, in fact, we should and we must. It just means it's easier when we are young and just starting out because we face less risk and have more trust.

As we gain more experiences and create interpretations and perceptions, we tend to allow these thoughts, and our feelings about these thoughts, to rule our current reality. This in turn helps us to construct our present and future life, for better or for worse.

I didn't think about this type of stuff back then and in the back of my mind I always knew that my time spent in school and in sport were worthwhile experiences. I was learning valuable skills and lessons about how to deal with adversity and these lessons would somehow serve me when I "went out into the world."

"Life is 10% what happens to you and 90% how you react to it" *Charles R. Swindoll*

My reaction to this parental mandate was to make sure I pleased both my parents and myself at the same time. I teamed up with my best friend Len and we started our own parking lot striping business. We were able to get some contracts from Len's dad to get started and we asked business owners if they would like their stripes freshened up. This created a snowball effect, which enabled us to keep busy all through college. We made enough to pay our tuition and saved the rest for travelling during the December break at school. I was able to finish university, which pleased my parents to no end, and I did make enough to be able to travel to the Bahamas, Europe, Australia and Hawaii. This wet my deep-seated hunger to experience the world and see what it was like outside of my small town.

When I graduated, I told my mom (my parents had split up when I was eighteen years old) that I was going to go to Australia to see if I could somehow get a job and live there for a while. I had a simple goal. I wanted to prove to my friends, my family, and myself, that I could "make it on my own."

My back-up plan was simple. My flight ticket was good for one year. I could make one stop on my way back home and still get back to my hometown within that year. Back then, long haul flights from USA to

Australia needed to stop in Hawaii to refuel before continuing on their journey. My ticket routed through Honolulu, Hawaii and Denver, Colorado.

If I failed to get a job or find an opportunity to support myself in Australia then I felt like I could always stop off in Hawaii and get a job and maybe start my Master's Degree. The bonus of living in Honolulu would be that I could also learn to surf. If, however, I decided to stop off in Denver, Colorado, then I could always do the same and follow one of my newfound passions, snow skiing. I learned to ski (self-taught, not a pretty picture) in Austria on one of my trips to Europe.

"Always have a Plan B and make sure it's just as appealing but in a different way than Plan A."

My Plan "A" was risky. I didn't have a work visa for Australia and I didn't have enough money to last for more than a few months. My back-up plan was not as exotic but I knew I could get a job on American soil and still be living in a cool city and doing fun things.

As it turns out, I ended up not getting a job in Australia, at least, not in the traditional sense. Because I didn't have a work visa, all the companies that interviewed me told me I needed a work permit first before they could even consider hiring me. They said I needed to be sponsored prior to my arrival and that they didn't have a program for doing that.

Sponsorship involves proving that your position on offer could not be filled by an Australian. This meant that I needed to have specialist knowledge and/or experience. At only twenty-three years of age, I certainly had neither of these fresh out of university with a Bachelors of Arts degree in Economics and International Business.

I ended up getting the traditional backpacker's job selling paintings door to door for commission only. Wow, what an experience that was! I was told that the best way to sell these paintings was to tell the potential customers that you were the actual artist and that you were working on behalf of the "Starving Artists Association." We were also encouraged to mention that the proceeds from the paintings would be going to the association's up and coming event being held at Darling Harbour.

I got caught out pretty quickly trying to use this tactic. Someone asked me what type of paints I used. When I replied, "oils," with a bit of uncertainty in my voice. The customer immediately countered with, "Wow, because this looks exactly like you used water colors to me." Of course, I proceeded to make another elaborate lie about how new technology was developed to make oil based paint look almost exactly like watercolor. Needless to say, this approach didn't sell any paintings and made me feel like a phony so I dropped it straight away.

My new approach was to start by telling the truth. I was a traveller and wanted to pay my way around Australia. I asked if they could take a few moments to browse through the prints and see if something grabbed their eye. This approach felt better, more natural, and I could move quickly between doors and customers.

During my time using this "new method" of

working, my team leader stopped me and told me I was doing it all wrong. I needed to slow down and get inside each house. It sounded like I needed literally to use the 'ol, "put your foot in the door" technique. I was going through too many houses, what I came to understand later was referred to as "burning up territory".

My own method was pretty simple at the time.

Step 1: Knock on the door. Ask people if they had a few moments to look at this amazing artwork.
Step 2: Stay on the front porch so as to not waste time. Flip through the prints quickly.
Step 3: See if anything piqued their interest then ask for the order.

This crazy, simple, logical, truthful, three-step system worked and it allowed me to sell three paintings in about three hours. I ended up being the "high roller" of the evening. On the way home in the crowded station wagon I was informed that the "high roller" of the day had to buy the crate of beer for the group – twenty-four bottles. *This is my reward*, I thought. *There goes my profit for the evening.* To make matters worse when we got back to the office that night I was informed that I would not be paid for the paintings I sold until the customers' cheques cleared. Needless to say, I was not in the least bit happy with how this company worked and knew I should start looking for something else if I wanted to stay in Australia.

It was clear that this company would not provide me with the best opportunity to make money and stay in

Australia. I figured I could do much better some other way.

Every new experience brings valuable lessons and mine were just beginning to unfold.

My Business Lessons:

1. The Law of Averages works. Each "no" does bring you closer to a "yes" if you're willing to work hard and be sincere about your offering. I am not suggesting that this is the only way to sell a product or service but at least in the beginning of my sales career I found out that something did work and could be relied on to make sales and make money. I now understood the expression, "It's a numbers game."

2. Companies have cultures. I didn't feel comfortable in this company's culture. The trainers and leaders had no interest in listening to my logic or me. In fact they didn't train me at all, they just threw me out in the field with an armload of paintings and expected me to sell by stretching the truth. They had not explained their terms of payment policies or that the new guy would be expected to buy everyone drinks on the way home every evening. I felt like I had been taken advantage of.

3. Opportunity cost: My economics training kicked in. I was much better off spending my time searching for a new opportunity than to persist with the current one.

The next day my shared accommodation roommate asked me to drop him off somewhere for an interview. I was the only one in the house who had a car. It wasn't the best of wheels but for $800.00 it was the best investment I could make on my limited budget. I figured having a car would make it easier to find opportunities to learn, grow and make some money. I just had to figure

8

out how to shift gears with my left hand and drive o wrong side (left side) of the road.

As I drove my friend to the interview and droppe him off in front of the building, I can remember thinking that this company seemed much more professional than my current one. It was situated in a pristine new white building with blue awnings. When he got home I asked him how the interview went and he responded with a begrudging, "Aw, mate its some sort of sales job. They offered me a trial day but I don't think I'm gonna go."

I thought if he's not going to take it then maybe I could somehow take his place? "Do you mind if I give them a call?" I quickly asked.

"No worries, mate," he responded like a true blue Aussie.

I immediately gave the company a call. The response was amazing! The pleasant voice on the other end of the phone sounded genuinely excited that I was applying for work. *This is certainly promising*, I thought. Debbie (the voice on the other end) had natural people skills. She made me "feel special" with her enthusiasm. She made me feel like I had a good shot at getting started with her "fun" sounding company.

Business Lesson 1

Pretend that everyone has a sign over his or her head that says, *Make Me Feel Special.* If you can get your team to tap into that, you've got the best chance for continual success.

I could barely wait for my interview the next day. I was already dreaming and hoping that this might be the place that would give me the opportunity I wanted. As previously mentioned, I had already visited quite a few established companies for interviews and their response was always the same: "I'm sorry, there's nothing we can do for you unless you have a work visa?"

For this reason I had all but given up on the idea of getting a traditional job in the traditional way while I was in Australia. I had inadvertently created my own "Catch 22" situation by not doing my homework before I left home. Catch 22 was a famous novel written by Joseph Heller, the title of which became a phrase to describe a puzzle that is impossible to solve.

In hindsight I should have done a bit more research before making the decision to go to Australia. But sometimes being young, bold and shortsighted can work in your favor. In my case, I was determined to "make my own way" in the world. I didn't see the importance of planning too far ahead. My risky approach somehow created the luck and synchronicity I needed to land an opportunity.

CHAPTER 1 LEARNING POINTS:

LIFE and BUSINESS WISDOM

How you respond to challenges and adversity will determine your fate – Be sure to take the route that challenges you to grow and move out of your comfort zone. Remember: you can always go back home.

Every new opportunity offers a chance to learn new things, new skills and meet new people – always give "yes" the highest weight and consideration. "Yes" is always more powerful than "NO." No is an end point.

Honesty in your sales interactions is paramount to build a successful future – If the company or products you represent don't honor honesty then leave immediately because things for them and you will eventually end up badly if you don't. Your time and honor are precious things. Respect that.

Less analysis and more action often reaps higher dividends – Follow Tom Cruise's advice in "Risky Business" Sometimes you just gotta say "what the _ _ _ _!"

CHAPTER 2

The "Power of Empowerment"

The next day I couldn't wait to go to my interview. My imagination was stirring and I was very excited. I made sure I arrived fifteen minutes early. I wore the only suit that I had packed before I left home. I was on a mission to prove to myself and my friends back home that I could make it on my own and was not a typical back packer. I was determined not to go home with my tail between my legs. I had my one-year ticket and, by God, I was going to last at least one year.

When I hit the intercom buzzer and the enthusiastic voice welcomed me to come up the stairs, I got really pumped up. Debbie worked her charm once again and made me feel special.

She gave me an application form and, even though I had a resume, told me to grab a seat and fill out the form. She said I could give my resume to the manager in the interview but the application form needed to be complete for the company's records. I noticed that there were a few other people coming up the stairs and the office was buzzing with a positive energy.

As I diligently filled out the application form, I wasn't able to pay much attention to the rest of the applicants. I did notice, however, that I was the only one dressed in a suit. I felt a bit out of place but it was too late to back out.

I was relieved when the manager came out from behind his partition dressed in a sharp-looking suit. He was as enthusiastic as his office assistant and welcomed me with the same open manner.

Business Lesson 2

"The example you set is the example you get."

This gentleman, named Chris, was young, confident and enthusiastic. He appeared as if he was extremely successful. His positive manner was uplifting so I couldn't help but match his energy. He asked me about myself and my background and what brought me to Australia.

His questions were not much different than my previous interviews but the manner and order in which he asked them was. The questions seemed like mere formality. The real purpose of the interview was to get to know me and discover what made me tick.

It felt good. I felt like I was special and important and the fact that I was inexperienced didn't seem to be the deciding factor. In fact, he seemed more interested in my goals and ambitions and knowing if I was willing to learn.

He asked me if I was interested in management. I said, "Yes, of course."

"Have you managed people before?" he wanted to know. Man, that was a killer question and it really floored me. I would be forced to tell the truth and my veil of confidence was immediately shattered.

"No, I haven't," I answered. I have only managed myself." My only two work-related experiences before this were a landscaping business that my buddy and I had run just after high school to make enough money to travel to Europe, and the fledgling parking lot striping business that we set up to pay our way through university.

Business Lesson 3

"Build-Break-Build." Build up their confidence (give measured and insightful compliment). Break them down a bit with your constructive criticism (give lesson or coaching tip). Build their confidence back up again (give more reassurance).

I felt like my chance at succeeding here was slipping away. I felt like my blood was draining into my feet and my brain was starting to slow down. Then Chris said, "No problem. Let me ask you a question. Do you think you could learn how to manage people if I taught you? We do have a management training program that I might be able to get you into, that is, if you get the position and can prove yourself in the sales area."

"Yes! I'm sure I can learn, err I mean 'no', I know I can learn how to manage people if I'm given the chance and the right training." Inside I was thinking, *Wow! YES! This is unbelievable, a much bigger opportunity than I ever expected has just presented itself.* My previous experience was a blessing and my honesty pulled me through. I didn't try to lie or bluff my way into this position and I was being awarded with a chance – a chance to grow, to learn, to develop and be a part of something.

Chris was only twenty-two years old and on his way to becoming a remarkable entrepreneur. He had skipped the University route and ended up becoming a millionaire by the time he was twenty-three. He knew how to think big. He'd mastered the skill of sharing his thoughts, energy, motivation, and money by genuinely giving people an opportunity to build their own businesses thus expanding his own organization. I was quickly absorbing this positive vibe and learning the "power of empowerment."

He then asked me the question that I didn't want to have to answer – if I had a visa to work in Australia. I knew I had to tell the truth but I also knew by now that I should phrase it in a way that made it seem easy and possible for me to get one. I explained to him that I had done some research and all I needed was a company to sponsor me. He said, "Okay… well, let's first see if you can get working with us and then we'll look into the possibility of sponsorship."

This was exactly what I was hoping to hear. I just needed a small break to get my life going in this amazing city of Sydney.

Opportunity is just a chance, and that's all I needed at this point in my life. I was scheduled to go for my "observation day" with this company on the next day. This would be a trial day for me to look at the business and the company to look at me but I was also committed to going to my other job at 4:00 p.m. the same day.

I asked if it was possible to cut the observation day a bit short so I could still go to my current job. I assured

Chris that I didn't like the other job as they seemed unprofessional and also because I wasn't sure that they would pay me for my sales. However, they were expecting me to be there and I didn't want to break my commitment.

He said he understood and would make an exception on this occasion. Little did I know, he was impressed with my professionalism and saw potential in me that I hadn't yet seen in myself.

CHAPTER 2 LEARNING POINTS

LIFE and BUSINESS WISDOM

Keep searching until you find a company culture that inspires and excites you. If you don't find it then make it your goal to influence your current culture to the best of your ability or take it upon yourself to start your own business.

Be enthusiastic in business & Life: Enthusiasm, passion and positive energy acts as a magnet attracting more positive people and events to your business and life.

Be honest and don't just tell the truth - Sell the truth.

CHAPTER 3

A "Trial Day" that changed the course of my life

My mind was racing after my interview with Chris and I could barely get to sleep that evening. I was thinking, dreaming, hoping that this job would be my ticket. I wanted more than anything to get this chance to start learning new skills and show the world what I could do.

You can imagine my shock when I showed up for my observation day (Trial Day) and was asked to wait in the lobby with another fifteen people who clearly were there for the same thing – a chance to get a job with this brand new company with massive growth plans.

The Managing Director, Chris came out from behind his partitioned office that was crammed full of what appeared to be his staff hovering over his big black desk. He was energetic, charismatic and exuded an unmistakable confidence in his business. *Nothing has changed since my interview*, I thought. He jumped right in with his introductory speech.

"Good morning everyone and congratulations for getting past the first interview. We interviewed fifty people yesterday and short-listed each of you for an observation day today. This is a chance for you to see what we do but it's also a chance for us to evaluate you throughout the day. Unfortunately, we can't give everyone a position. We are looking for six people to get started with us today and we will be assessing you at the end of the day with a test and a final interview. Good luck everyone and I'll see you at the end of the day."

He proceeded to introduce each applicant to various staff members called "trainers" and asked us to observe, learn and ask questions throughout the day. He would see us in the evening for our final interview between 5:00 and 6:00 p.m.

Had he forgotten that I had to be at my other job in Surry Hills at 4:00 p.m.? *Should I interrupt him and blow my chances of being one of the six people?* My brain was spinning but my heart said to interrupt him and tell him the truth. So I did and I could see that he had forgotten. It's not surprising if he had interviewed fifty people the previous day.

"Oh yeah, right... now I remember that you mentioned that yesterday. Sure, Steve make sure you get Dominic back for his final interview by 3:30 so he can still get to his other job by 4:00."

Personal Lesson

Tell the truth no matter what. Relationships built on little lies from the beginning are doomed to fail long term.

Steve was amazing. He had so much self-confidence and seemed to really enjoy what he was doing. Remember at this stage, I still didn't know what we were going to do. I knew the company was a wholesale company and I knew I was going to have to do some form of sales. That was about it.

I was about to find out. After we were introduced, we walked out of the office and away from the gathering crowd of people.

Steve then asked me if I had eaten anything for breakfast. I said I had. He said, "Good, 'cause you see those guys there?" He gestured toward another group. "They always run across the road after the meeting to grab a bite but what I like to do is to get out to my territory before them and start making sales before they even finish their late breakfast." Then he added (and I love this), "But if you get started with us, you can choose whether you join them for breakfast or head straight out to your territory. It's up to you."

When we finally got to his car, he explained how the day would unfold. He told us where we would go and what we would do. He mentioned that I could ask him more questions in the car. Was I ready to head out? For sure, I was. I was intrigued and couldn't wait to see what we were going to do and how we were going to do it.

On the drive to the industrial area, Steve asked me about myself and what had brought me to Australia, what did I study at "uni" (Australian slang for university) and how I found out about the company. He asked me personal questions about my family and was interested in my travels through Europe.

He shared his story with me, too. I found out that he was an accountant and had left a big firm in Melbourne to go travelling to Canada. He told me how he had got started with the business in Vancouver as a traveller just to make some cash but when he had heard that the company was looking to expand to Australia, he just had to be a part of it.

He knew that this concept would be successful in his own country. He convinced his manager in Vancouver to find out whom he needed to contact in order to be a part of the Australian team. With his excellent sales performance and his Australian citizenship it didn't take much convincing to be selected for the Australian team.

Steve ended up meeting Chris at a company meeting and the plans were laid for the big company expansion "Down Under."

Business Lesson 4

Great businesses are built through building strong relationships in the early days and keeping the original dream alive. Having fun and making money can be mutually inclusive.

I still didn't know exactly what we were going to do but I was thoroughly enjoying my conversation with Steve. He had left a corporate job and a steady career for what we were about to do. I thought that it must be something really special for a guy like this to want to leave a secure future.

When we got to the industrial area and found a parking spot, we got out of the car and Steve went to his trunk and grabbed a small duffel bag. He opened the bag and pulled out some flat silver and white boxes.

He opened one of the boxes and I caught a glimpse of what looked like close to a dozen black and gold pens. They looked like Cross pens. He then took one of the pens out and handed it to me.

"What do you think? Pretty cool, huh?" They are a Cross replica. "They're great quality at a really cheap price. We import these form Hong Kong. In a normal shop they would retail between fifteen and twenty bucks but because we buy so many of them that we can offer them to the businesses for only $5.00 each. That's way more than fifty percent off retail. What do you think?" He answered before I could respond. "Pretty good, huh?"

Is he pitching me? Good strategy, I thought. Now I understood what it was to be on the receiving end.

"What we're going to do now is to go into these businesses and pitch them. I want you to stay right next to me because that's the only way for you to learn. You don't need to say anything, except you do need to smile and say, "Hi". How does that sound?" I nodded and we were off.

He told me he had three objectives and his primary goal was not necessarily to make sales. His objectives were:

1) Test market his products and get people's opinions.

2) Show me and teach me how to do the business.

3) Make sure I passed the test and final interview by the end of the day so I could get started with the company.

It was a good thing he explained it in exactly that way because for the next five hours we went in and out of every single company in our chosen area. It didn't matter if it was retail or industrial, we went inside and pitched the first pair of eyes that greeted us. Steve was pitching receptionists, factory workers, sole proprietors, retail assistants and anyone else that inadvertently crossed our path. After all this energy and effort, Steve managed to sell absolutely NOTHING! His gross sales of these magnificent pens were exactly zero!

I have to admit that I really admired Steve's unwavering confidence, work ethic and enthusiasm, especially in the face of this kind of rejection. He just kept going. We didn't stop to eat lunch and my stomach was growling but I didn't dare ask because I desperately wanted to be one of the few to get selected. I didn't know how the company made it's money but it was pretty clear to me that we wouldn't get paid to just walk around and show people our products and get their opinions on it.

His pitch never wavered and he always asked people to buy in the dozens. He told prospective customers that if they bought twelve he would throw one in for free. After seeing all this rejection, I mentioned to Steve that maybe he should consider just selling one pen for five dollars instead of asking people to buy twelve at a time. I didn't really get a response from him other than his insistence that the day was going really well.

He kept mentioning all the people who seemed to show some interest and might buy at a future date. He then countered my question with a question of his own. He asked me if I knew the five steps of a sale because it would be on the test at the end of the day.

This got my brain re-focused on the job at hand and kept me from questioning his work methods. I now had to try to figure out his sales pitch. What was he doing and when? What were the pieces of the process?

I was thinking about the five steps. It seemed more like three to me. You say, "hi". That was Step One. Step Two is to tell a bit about your company and some crap about the product. Step Three: Ask them if they want to grab a dozen.

He didn't seem too impressed with my "crap" remark. I felt funny for saying it. Here I thought I could relax a bit with him and that we were buddies and he got me back on my toes. I remembered that I was on a full day job interview and realized that maybe I was not as sharp as I thought. Just because he wasn't selling anything at all didn't mean that I had the right to start acting cool.

Business Lesson 5

Business is about taking control and being bold. It's important to keep people on their toes and challenge them mentally, otherwise they won't respect you and you lose control.

Towards the end of the day we walked into an industrial unit and ended up engaged in a conversation with the owner. Steve pulled out a new twist on his pitch that I hadn't heard yet.

He mentioned, "What most Companies are doing is getting the pens engraved with their company name on them and giving them out to their best customers as gifts." I noticed that the gentleman kept looking at the pen while Steve was explaining this idea. Then Steve made his close. "If you're looking to grab at least a hundred then I can get them engraved for you for free".

The potential buyer didn't flinch at this suggestion. Steve mentioned that he would show him a sample of what it would look like and then the gentleman could make up his mind if he wanted to order less than a hundred pens and pay for the engraving or take the hundred and get it for free.

He took the pen out of the man's hand and put it back in the box and told him we would drop by in an hour or so to show him a sample of an engraved pen. The potential customer agreed and we were off to pitch more people and continue on our "test marketing" journey to thus far zero sales.

I was getting hungry and Steve just carried on with a maddening perseverance. I didn't dare ask if we were going to stop for lunch. I was well aware that Steve would be reporting back to his manager all his observations and opinions about me.

I let my stomach growl as we carried on. In and out of businesses, pitching secretaries, factory workers, retail employees in shopping malls. Steve's attitude was amazing. He never stopped pitching big - Buy-twelve-and-get-one-free -Still no sales.

I was looking for a crack in his armor, a sign of giving up or changing his pitch or style. I found no signs of resignation, no signs of quitting or giving up. In fact, I was in utter shock when he turned to me and said, "Well, the day's going just as planned. As I explained in the beginning my goal was not to so much sell but to do test marketing and create awareness for our products. So far, so good, in fact, I wanted to cover this entire industrial area and we've almost completed our goal."

Business Lesson 6

Always display an amazing attitude while "on show", whether training, leading, working, or managing. It's infectious and rubs off on everyone around you.

We rounded a corner and found a small shopping mall. Lo, and behold, inside the mall was a small engraving kiosk. Steve asked the guy how much he would charge to engrave the pen and the guy said about five bucks. Steve said, "What if I could give you a bulk order of a hundred and continued to give you more business? We're a large importer and there's a huge demand from our customers to engrave their companies' names on the pens and give them to their best customers."

The guy's eyes lit up. He dropped his price to a dollar a pen. *Wow*, I thought, *everything is negotiable*. This really opened my eyes to the world of business. I was so used to just paying the retail price on the sticker.

Growing up in the suburbs and going to shopping malls meant that I was conditioned to look at what I wanted, find out the sticker price and then figure out how to get, make or obtain the money. If I was lucky I could find it on sale.

This idea of barter and negotiation based on collaboration in the future with a total stranger was mind blowing. A new world was opening up in front of my eyes. My college education suddenly seemed worthless. My economics degree was theory only. This was practical application and real business. My motivation was edging higher and higher.

In my eyes, Steve was a true leader. He was a 28-year-old accountant who had quit the corporate "Promised Land", a guaranteed, secured future with prestige and a huge pension. He freaked out his friends and family when he decided to quit his career and backpack through Canada only to find an opportunity to sell products business to business for commission only. Of course, at this stage in the day, I'm still not too sure how I will be paid if I get selected.

He followed his urge to go his own way and decided not to take the normal, predictable career path. He wanted more and needed to experience more. His worst-case scenario was to go back home and find a job as an accountant. What did he have to lose? How much could he gain and grow personally and professionally by stepping out into the unknown?

You have three choices in life: Grow, blow or flow. Let me explain.

Grow means that when you are presented with a challenge you face it and discover what you can learn from it.

Blow means you can choose to quit, turn and run.

Flow means you stick around, observe the challenge and meander through.

I can probably blame or thank my mother for my life's journey and amazing experiences. On my thirteenth birthday, she gave me a poster and wrote me a nice note

27

encouraging me to hang the poster on my bedroom wall. Like a good son, I did as I was told. The poster featured a picture of a forest with some footsteps in the snow. The caption read, "Do not follow where the path leads, rather go where there is no path and leave a trail."

Inspiring words. Later, I was to find out that the original phrase is attributed to Ralph Waldo Emerson but the poster makers, in order to avoid copyright issues, re-worded it a bit. The original quote says, "Do not go where the path may lead, go instead where there is no path and leave a trail."

Isn't this an inspiring way to go through life? Whoever accomplished anything great by following the path of another? We are all original souls destined to think and feel and have our own personal experiences. We can follow and learn from others but there always comes a time to break away and chase our deepest dreams and our treasured thoughts. There is a deep need within each one of us to connect with that feeling of personal triumph and personal success.

We know if we're on that path or if we're playing it safe and shrinking from challenge. We know when we're not growing and learning. We don't usually need to be told.

Unbeknownst to me, on this observation day, my biggest fear in life was about to rear its ugly head. I was going to be forced to deal with this demon for better or for worse.

My ambition was on a crash course with one of my life's biggest fears – Public Speaking.

I still didn't have this job yet and I wouldn't come

face to face with my next challenge for a couple of days. I kept looking at my watch because I needed to get back for the final interview and I had already promised my current "opportunity givers" at the Acme Art Selling Company that I would be there at 4:30.

I wanted so badly to quit that job but it was all I had at the moment and needed to make some money. I was incurring expenses and burning through my savings at a pretty good pace. Remember, my goal was to stay away from home for at least a year without having to go back to my hometown and previous way of living. I was on a mission to prove to my friends, family and myself that I could do it on my own.

Steve noticed my edginess and knew that he had made a promise to get me back to the office. He also knew that he hadn't sold anything or told me that this job was commission only. The pressure was on him to succeed and little did I know that his career goals were dependent upon building a sales team. He needed me to see the sales, he needed me to be motivated about doing this work so he could build his own team and get his own office.

Business Lesson 7

Keep relaxed and in the flow. The pressure is not on you; it's always on the customer to solve their challenges or issues. Your job is to create massive want and desire. You do this by presenting your product or service in the most inspiring way and demonstrating all the powerful benefits of ownership.

We headed back to the engraver and grabbed the engraved pen with the company's name inscribed on it. The guy did an excellent job and I was interested to see how well the potential client would receive this. We hurried back to the business in hopes of catching the owner there. We walked in and Steve presented the engraved pen.

He held the box in a certain way as to hide the engraved pen until the right moment so the customer could just catch a glimpse of the engraving but not see exactly what was written on it. Then Steve slowly brought the pen forward and placed it in the businessman's hand and said, "Well! What do you think about that? The engraver did a great job on it don't you think? So how many did you want to pick up today? Is twelve dozen enough?"

The man hesitated for what seemed like an eternity while Steve just remained silent before he replied, "Well, I'm not sure if I could use that many."

"Like I said, if you grab over a hundred then I will toss in the engraving for free, as well for each dozen you purchase, I will throw in a pen for free. So that would be a hundred forty-four pens, plus twelve for free."

At this stage the guy got a bit confused and said, "Sorry, how much was that again, for the lot?" What's weird is that Steve had never mentioned the price, only that we were importers and were selling products at wholesale prices. He explained that we were saving local businesses money because they normally can't get wholesale prices unless they buy in bulk. If we sold each business in the area a dozen pens then we would still be able to give wholesale prices and make our margins.

By now we knew for sure he was interested. He got a little ego boost seeing his company name engraved on the pen. You could almost see his imagination moving forward, thinking how great it would be to give these pens to his preferred customers.

Business Lesson 8

Always look for at least one of these three buying signals:

1. The customer responds by acknowledging your presence. (If you've ever done Business-to-Business B2B cold calling then you know about this one)

2. You can get your product or at least a brochure into their hands. (Engagement)

3. They ask questions. (Showing interest)

This customer has definitely qualified (second phase of selling process) himself by doing all three. Steve still played it out a bit more by explaining that the pens retailed individually for $7.50 but we sell a dozen for $60.00 plus throw in a free pen which cuts the cost down to $4.61 per pen. The engraver charges $2.50 per pen but we promised to throw that in for free if he grabbed over a hundred pens so the customer would be saving nearly $500.00 in the deal.

By now, the customer is not even considering his option to purchase fewer than a hundred pens. He only wants to know how much it would set him back for the one hundred and fifty-six pens. He also fell in love with seeing his company name inscribed on the pen in gold letters. Steve mentioned that most companies are giving them out to their preferred customers. Now he feels that he's also not alone in making this purchase. This is known as social proofing in the sales industry.

The customer just sat there in silence obviously thinking whether or not he should make the commitment, Steve surely didn't want the impulse to die so he quickly and confidently said, "I can get them to the printers now and they can be delivered to you by tomorrow afternoon."

He was gambling a bit because he hadn't discussed this with the engraver but that's all a part of going for it and making things happen. Steve closed him, "Like I said, you would normally pay close to $1500.00 for twelve dozen engraved pens but I'll let you have the lot with free engraving for $720. That's way less than half price. How would you like to pay, cash or cheque?"

The customer looked up from staring at the professionally engraved pen and said, "If you'll wait a minute I can go and grab the cash."

I was in shock. Steve had held out all day, kept pitching, never second-guessed his approach and kept his attitude positive. We drove back to the office with no pens left because we dropped them off at the engravers and we had $720.00 in cash. What an amazing experience that was for me.

On the drive back to the office, Steve just acted normal and asked me if I had any questions that I wanted to ask him before I took the test and final interview. He told me I needed to know about the 5 steps to a sale and the 7 steps to success. I asked him if he could run over them again for me as we headed back for the test and final interview.

My stomach was still growling and Steve finally mentioned that he was sorry about not stopping but he said he sometimes gets too caught up in his work that he forgets to stop for lunch. I said "no worries". It was a great day and I appreciated him taking the time to show me how he works.

CHAPTER 3 LEARNING POINTS:

LIFE and BUSINESS WISDOM

When leading and training people always maintain your course of action – "No matter what"

In Sales, The "Law of averages" works even and up until the last call of the day. Believe in it and let it work magic for you.

The sales process works. You must stick with the system and trust in the successful outcome.

You're always being watched by your colleagues and customers, keep on a brave face and show your confidence and charisma while working. This will increase your chances of success by an immeasurable factor.

There is always a buyer. Persevere and you are guaranteed to find them.

80% of salespeople fail to become superstars because they don't develop a proper sales process /conversation with a clearly defined close or request for an order.

Money is the by-product of belief, confidence, perseverance, passion and enthusiasm. Make sure you keep developing these qualities in your professional life. They will serve you well.

CHAPTER 4

Mentors Matter Deeply – Some you only meet once very briefly

On the way back to the office, I had the opportunity to get to know Steve a bit more. I love stories about people's lives and they're big "why" when making life decisions. Especially those decisions that have the potential to change the course of one's life. I wasn't particularly wise at twenty-three years of age and fresh out of university. I did, however, have some guts and I was making changes to my life by deciding to stay in Australia until either my year was completed or I screwed up and ran out of money.

Just before I embarked on my Australian journey, I had lined up an interview with a large American Fortune 500 company. One of my best college buddies, Doug Thompson, had graduated a semester before me and had already been working there for several months. He knew a few of the Vice-Presidents and was able to put in a good word on my behalf and organized an interview.

I was so busy running my fledgling parking lot and road striping business that I didn't have much time to think about my career options. We were doing so well and with the addition of some lucrative federal highway and road striping contracts my business partner's dad was bringing in, I could already imagine a successful future continuing with our current business. Plus, I was having a great time working with my best friend along with the added perks of working outside and being our own bosses while travelling all over eastern Tennessee and Northern Georgia.

It wasn't until the last semester of my studies and knowing that I would have my degree in hand within six months that I started to think about other options. My friend, Doug, in Nashville seemed like he had a serious opportunity to grow with his corporate job. My mom also encouraged me to at least go for the interview and hear them out. So I did.

My experience in that interview was life changing on a couple of levels. I got the chance to share my interview story with Steve as he told his story about his dissatisfaction with the slow, boring, predictable corporate future from which he was highly motivated to escape.

By the time I went for the interview, the Corporate Vice-President, Mr. Sherman, was close to retirement. I had already booked my flight tickets to Australia. So, in some ways, our destinies were bound to conflict. He had spent his entire life working at the same company. He had worked his way up to his current position and was only about a year away from retirement. He was a smart and accomplished man. Our interview was planned for the early morning and then we would go for lunch in the afternoon.

This was my first ever interview so I didn't know what to expect. I don't think we ever talked about it in any of my classes and my parents never discussed any type of interview etiquette, so I was unprepared, to say the least. I only knew that The Corporation was a well-known retail Brand and I had worn their undergarments over the years. What was there to know? They make underwear, right?

Mr. Sherman was extremely knowledgeable and did most of the talking for the first two hours. We went through the history of cotton and I can remember him asking me some really strange questions that seemed really important for me to answer correctly.

His first question was, how many US soldiers died in WWI? I got that one really wrong and am still too embarrassed to even reveal my answer. Let's just say that I answered in five figures where I should have picked six figures to be closer to the accurate count.

Mr. Sherman seemed disturbed with my answer. He cleared his throat and gave me a shaming look before correcting my ridiculous answer. The next question should have been even trickier but my limited knowledge in American history actually served me well. Because I had so few historical names in my memory bank, I actually guessed correctly when he asked me who had surveyed the state of Virginia?

"George Washington," I suggested sheepishly.

Vice-president Sherman stared at me briefly over his horn rimmed glasses and said, "Right, well..." and then he carried on with his story about cotton and how his Corporation was an integral part of not only cotton but the entire history of America.

Two things happened in that interview that changed the course of my life. One was a lesson given to me by Mr. Sherman that has stuck with me to this day.

The first thing happened about half way through the interview and convinced me I was probably in the wrong place. Mr. Sherman was interrupted by one of his junior staff members. At least I assumed he was junior staff by the way he was treated.

The young man had knocked on the door and asked politely if he could step into the office and grab a folder he needed from the side table. Mr. Sherman reluctantly agreed. It was clear he was not happy about the interruption but allowed this young man to get what he needed.

He then introduced us in a way that had a deep impact on me. He said, "I would like to introduce you to Dan. He's one of our account executives, who is smart enough to do what he's told. Isn't that right Dan?"

"Yes sir, Mr. Sherman," Dan replied.

Mr. Sherman then turned to look straight into my eyes and said, "We like 'yes men' around here, don't we. Dan?"

Dan replied, "Yes sir," He swiftly walked out of the office and quietly shut the door behind him.

As you might imagine, this incident had a profound effect on my lack of motivation, not only to avoid getting a job at this company but also to avoid corporate jobs all together. I interpreted that most Corporations with large organizations might all have a similar culture.

The second thing that happened after this incident was of my own making. I wanted to turn the tables and get to know my interviewer. He knew a lot about me – my education, my parents' occupations, and my reasons for thinking I was a good fit as a corporate sales executive. I genuinely wanted to know what a successful VP of a major corporation was going to do when he retired. I was able to sneak in the question between his long tirades about how wonderful his employer was.

It seemed to really strike a cord with him and I remember his eyes lighting up and his gestures becoming decidedly more animated as he told me that he was going to run his own small business. He asked me if I had ever noticed in some of the shopping malls the small booths sitting in the middle of the aisles? Yes, of course I had.

He asked if I had ever noticed any shoe repair booths? I thought about that then answered, "Oh yes, like Mr. Minit Shoe Repair."

"Yes," he replied, but "his" vision was to be distinct in other ways and he began to enthusiastically describe his plan for differentiation. He exuded passion and energy. I forgot I was in an interview and at some point he seemed to realize the same. He quickly regained his composure and continued on with his interview spiel.

This experience was a gift from Mr. Sherman. It completely motivated me to opt out of corporate America before I began. I had already run two companies since high school and didn't appreciate how lucky I was to work for myself until I met my interviewer. Thank you, Mr. Sherman. You saved me many years of drudgery and motivated me to attempt to create a different path for myself in a new country.

The nice thing about this interview is that it actually reduced my choices. I was no longer motivated to work at a big corporation. Believe it or not, sometimes having fewer choices makes life easier.

Steve inspired me with his story. It took him five years to break away from the corporate grind and find his dream opportunity. This example coupled with my recent interview with Mr. Sherman solidified my resolve to find my perfect opportunity and that opportunity was more than likely not with a big Corporation.

CHAPTER 4 LEARNING POINTS:

LIFE and BUSINESS WISDOM

Watch people's passionate and expressive energy closely. They can act as valuable signposts to guide you to make the right decisions concerning your life's direction.

Finding your Life's Vocation is as much about tweaking and limiting your choices as it is about imagining all the opportunities.

Never be afraid of asking questions – It's been said that the dumbest question is the one you never ask - So true.

CHAPTER 5

The Test and Final Interview

Steve parked the car and we headed towards the front door of the office building. Just before he opened the door Steve stopped me to say that he really enjoyed the day with me and that we would be heading upstairs so I could take the test and then go for the final interview. He asked me if I had any last minute questions before we headed up?

I told him I was ready and off we went. Because we were back earlier than normal there wasn't much activity in the office but there was still a buzz in the air with the few office staff that was around.

Debbie was there with a great big smile on her face as usual and asked me how my day was with Steve. She said I was lucky because Steve was a great trainer. I agreed as she handed me the two-page test and asked me grab a seat and to take my time filling it out.

Steve said he needed to go speak with the manager and would be out in a few minutes to check up on me.

The test wasn't as easy as I had expected. The questions were simple but I didn't want to appear stupid and write down any ridiculously wrong answers. Sure enough, the questions about the five and seven steps were on it but there were additional questions asking about why it is important to maintain a positive attitude throughout the day. Also, beyond the sales aspects, did I think I could master the sales skills well enough to teach and train others? And if so, why? I was asked to list three reasons, in order of importance, why customers would be motivated to purchase our products.

This took a bit of complex thought to construct the right answers in order to impress the manager. I hoped I might be able to seek a higher position from the get go.

Steve came back after about ten or fifteen minutes to check up on me. He noticed that I was not even half way through answering the questions. I was well aware that at this rate, I was definitely going to be late for my next appointment so he suggested I hustle up a bit.

All I could think was, *screw my next appointment*. I really need to focus on this test and get this job opportunity. I put my head down and focused on finishing the test and answering all the questions with the best of my knowledge, passion and intensity.

When I finally finished, Steve appeared from the manager's office, grabbed the clipboard, and folded the paper without looking at it. I thought this was extremely professional as there were a few questions on the test designed to glean information about the trainer, like: What did I like about him/her? What did I dislike? Were they highly motivated, sometimes motivated, or not motivated? Did I think they were confident in their ability to attain success?

Steve motioned for me to follow him into the manager's office and he would re-introduce me to Chris. He stopped just before he opened the door and said, "Look mate, I put in a good word for you but Chris is pretty tough on people and has to make the right decisions on who gets started with us today. It's up to you now."

Chris was sitting behind his big black desk and stood up when we entered the room. He immediately said," Hi Dom, how's it going? Come over and grab a seat." He remained standing until we shook hands and took our positions.

I noticed he still had his amazingly positive energy about him. He was dressed very professional, a bit like Charlie Sheen from the blockbuster movie Wall Street. He exuded an enthusiastic charm when engaged in conversation and spoke with an authority as if he'd been in business for many years. This seemed a bit surreal to me considering he didn't appear to be older than thirty.

He was a man on a mission and was extremely confident and passionate when he spoke about his vision for the company. He first asked me a few general questions about how my day was with Steve, what I thought about the sales and marketing side of the business and if I thought I could perform well in sales. He then jumped straight to the big questions, "Do you think you could manage and motivate other people?"

"Sure I could!" I said. I was excited beyond measure.

He asked me to tell him why he should offer me this position considering that he was considering fifteen people for the position. I told him that I was highly motivated to do the job and that I felt sure I could learn to manage and motivate others.

The answer seemed not to impress Chris. "Yeah, well, almost everyone says that. Is there anything else you can tell me?"

Man, I thought, *don't the challenges ever stop?* I had given him all the answers I thought I had inside me. Now he wants me to give him more?

My heart was racing and my mind seemed frozen, "I'm a great team player, I'll stick at my task until the job is done and I'm passionate to become a manager some day!" I said with as much passion and intensity as I could muster.

He paused, looked me in the eyes as he was making his decision about my future and said, "Dom, congratulations. I'd like to offer you a position in our company." He stuck out his hand for a shake and I was in. I couldn't believe my luck. This was a massive victory for me. I was so excited I could barely contain myself.

Chris smiled and said, "Let's go tell Steve." Steve was busy counting out his cash and talking to another sales rep in the lobby. He ran over to congratulate me and walk me out the door. We made arrangements to meet up on Monday for my 1st day of field training and I hurried off to my final appointment with the Acme D2D Painting Sales Company.

I can remember feeling elated and on top of my world as I drove downtown to Surry Hills. I couldn't wait to tell the "bit too cool" office manager that, unfortunately, I was unable to work that evening as I got another position with a firm in Alexandria. Also, I was anxious to find out when I could expect my money for the paintings I had already sold.

Like many sales managers he was used to hearing this story. People are always coming and going in commission-only sales jobs. He was also very smooth when he explained that he couldn't release my money yet because they were still waiting for the bank to clear the cheques I had submitted. Although I was clearly upset and felt that I was being given the run around, I was too excited to let this little setback get me down. I thanked him for the opportunity and cordially left the office with the agreement that I would come pick up my commissions in about a week. Little did I know my life was about to change so drastically that I would never get a chance to go back there for my small pittance.

Unbeknownst to me, I was about to be inspired by a plan that would encompass everything I had always dreamed of and would also be facing a personal showdown between my ambitious dreams of becoming rich and my massive fear of speaking in public.

Like most people I never really knew what I wanted to do when I grew up. I was always a bit jealous when I met people that were so focused and knew what career path they wanted to follow. They knew what to study, which groups to join, how many years of higher education before they would launch into their dream career.

Studies show that most of us unconsciously decide very early in life, generally before we're 10 years old what we are going to do when we grow up. In my case I can recall standing in my grandmother's front yard looking her straight the eyes and telling her that I was going to "be rich" when I grew up. I will never forget the shocked look on her face. I was about six or seven years old at the time. It is an extremely colorful and vivid memory but not a very specific career path. However, it does help explain why I was completely drawn into this "World's Greatest Opportunity."

"Whatever the mind can conceive and believe it can achieve." *Napoleon Hill*

I had the weekend off to get organized and prepare myself before starting my new career. Steve would be showing me the sales techniques and the manager, Chris, had already expressed an interest in teaching me how to manage people. I spent the weekend organizing my one bedroom, shared accommodation. I ironed my two dress shirts and hung them on the wall. I blew up my air mattress to the max in preparation for a good night's sleep before my big starting day.

I was so happy that my mom had taken me shopping just before I left Chattanooga. She bought me a suit just in case I had the chance to go for some decent job interviews during my travels.

I never liked the backpacking gig. In fact, whenever my best friend and I travelled we always used a tote bag instead of a backpack. We also decided that we would rather stay in a budget hotel or B&B rather than a backpackers' inn. I have always had a sort of anti-social proof streak about me. It ran through my musical tastes and my choice of travel bag.

I didn't have much to my name. I drove an $800.00 Holden Torana. I owned one suit and two dress shirts. I slept on an air mattress that had a slow leak in it and needed a bit of air before I lay down each night.

But I was happy, motivated and ready to go.

CHAPTER 5 LEARNING POINTS:

LIFE and BUSINESS WISDOM

Be true to yourself and your higher destiny will unfold accordingly.

Every day of your life is a new beginning – start where you are with what you have and put your best foot forward.

Great Opportunities are everywhere if you dare to open your eyes to see them, heart to trust them and mind to tune into the unlimited possibilities.

PART II

It only takes 21 days to learn the skills of a lifetime, establish the right work habits and create the momentum to achieve breakaway success — you can alter the course of your life if you're willing to commit to a personal success strategy and follow it diligently.

CHAPTER 6

My first day as a "suit" (aka. re-train day)

I came into the office fifteen minutes early wearing a shirt, tie, and my new blue suit. I was carrying my coffee and a newspaper. I had watched enough TV to know how a manager was meant to go to the office. I always wondered during my outdoor jobs of landscaping and parking lot striping what "the suits" did for their work. I was about to find out. Before I did, I was about to encounter my first office adversary.

When I came up the steps, I saw a few people milling around. I looked for Steve but he wasn't there yet. So I headed for one of the seats in the reception area. I sat down, opened my paper and started to read the headlines when suddenly I could feel a presence hovering over me.

"Hi. How are you?" the young man asked.

I peered over the top of my paper with a perturbed look on my face and said, "Good."

He ignored my glare and said, "Are you a new guy?"

"I suppose," I answered.

He told me his name was Zoran and that he was one of the trainers. "I don't think you'll be around very long," he informed me. Then he simply walked off, into the back of the office, and left me sitting there.

Where did that come from? I wondered. He hadn't given me any explanation about his comment.

It seemed so abrupt and out of left field that I didn't know how to respond. I rolled my eyes and went back to reading my paper. Still, it made me feel the same as the last comment Mr. Sherman had given me when I was finished my first corporate interview.

After we had spent half the day together, Mr. Sherman's conclusion had been that I was not the right fit for the company and that I should go to Australia like planned. *Thanks for the blessing,* I sarcastically thought at the time. He suggested that I get travelling out of my system and perhaps when I came back, I could give him a call. It was the corporate way of letting someone know they didn't make the grade. On my way out of his office he had asked, "Would you like some advice?"

I thought, *what the heck. I didn't get the job anyway so maybe his thoughts can serve me.* "Sure" I responded.

"When you come for a job as a salesman you should dress like a salesman," he advised.

I was naïve to corporate dress standards to know what he meant. I had shown up wearing a white shirt, a red and blue diagonally striped tie, grey dress pants and a blue blazer. I looked at my wardrobe and felt confused and compelled to ask for elaboration.

"Do you mind telling me what you mean?" I meekly asked.

"Your shoes." *My shoes?* I thought, as I peered down at my classic and well-worn brown suede Hush Puppies. At the time, I couldn't believe how superficial corporate America was. I'm sure it still is at certain corporations but that's not the point. I couldn't believe for the life of me why my shoes would make any difference to my massive potential and limitless future? Nevertheless, that was my big personal take away from my corporate interview.[1]

Before I left for Australia, my mom also lovingly bought me a new pair of winged brogues to go with my new blue suit. So I learned from my experiences and was ready for Round Two.

Now, here I was again, not knowing where I had gone wrong. My only hope was that this Zoran character was not an influential player in the office. Steve arrived just as my thoughts were drifting back to the headlines in the Sydney Morning Herald.

"Hey, Dom, you're here early," he said with a bit of a smirk. "You won't be needing the newspaper or coffee in the office and we don't sit down in the morning either?"

Oh, I thought. *Now Zoran's advice is starting to make sense.*

"Let's get stuck in and I'll show you around the office real quick and then explain to you how the office runs in the morning," he said. "Chris is the owner of the business; you were in his office on Friday." He introduced me to Sue. "She's the head administrator and you already met Debs, who is the eyes and ears of the office, making sure everything runs smoothly.

Be nice to her because she's the one who will help

---

[1] At a later date when the shoe was on the other foot, so to speak, and my job was to hire, train and recruit top sales talent, I always judged a person by their attitude and ambition rather than their attire. I spent a fortune on shoes and suits for my trainees and created many top performers because of my initial investment.

you with your merchandise and settle-ups at the end of the day."

We then headed into the meeting room section of the office. There were only partitions set up around office desks, no walls, as there was about two thousand square feet of open-plan office space.

The area in the back was where everyone gathered. It was obvious that only certain people were allowed to talk to Chris, who was situated behind the partition.

It was around 7:20 in the morning and already the place was buzzing. People were laughing, music was blaring in the background, and everyone was standing up, moving around and talking enthusiastically with each other.

I had never experienced anything like this and was really getting excited about my new opportunity.

Steve explained that the morning was structured like this:

7:00 - 7:15 Trainers arrive and get their merchandise.

7:15 - 7:30 Trainers attend a meeting with the manager.

7:30 - 7:45 Merchandisers arrive, get merchandise and start pitching with each other.

7:45 - 8:00 Crew meetings.

8:00 - 8:15 Impact meeting (run by top trainer or office manager).

8:15 - 8:45 Morning meeting.

8:45 - 9:00 Trainers meet their observations.

(interviewees asked to come in for a trial day)

9:00 - Everyone hits the field.

Wow, I thought. *No time for reading the newspaper and enjoying a coffee here.*

The rest of the morning was a blur. There were about twenty people in the office, pitching (practicing a mock sales pitch with each other), laughing, and getting their consignment of merchandise. People started splitting up into their crew meetings and we got the low-down on whom the new people were and who had sold well the day before.

Then Steve broke away from our group, turned down the music, and screamed to the top of his voice, "Hey everybody, who wants an impact?"

Most of the people in the office responded by yelling and clapping. "We want an Impact! We want an Impact! We all want an impact! Oh, we all want an impact, so tell us Steve, baby!" Everyone shouted, punching his or her fist in the air and crowding around Steve as he began his impact lesson.

He talked about why we should always pitch big because you never know when you run across a customer who wants to buy more than one pen. I thought, *see, you can sell just one pen at a time.*

He went on to say that if you ran across a customer who has the means and potential to buy a hundred pens, but you as the salesperson were of the small-minded habit of pitching prospects to buy only one pen at a time, then you would still make the sale but the customer would probably only buy one pen instead of the one hundred he could use. Therefore, we should always pitch a big amount first so we wouldn't lose out on bulk orders. Considering that I had seen Steve in action on my observation day doing exactly that, I took notice.

Business Lesson 9

"Monkey see - monkey do," meaning show me how to do something first then you can tell me what you did and it will stick in my memory not the other way around.

I felt proud to be on Steve's team, watching him stand up in front of the whole office and share his knowledge. He spoke with flare and enthusiasm and had tons of self-confidence.

After the impact session, it was time for Chris to come up and speak. Before he did, there was another introduction song to sing. When Steve finished he yelled, "Who wants a meeting?" We all yelled, including me now, because I got the gist of the proceedings. "We want a meeting! We want a meeting! Oh, we all want a meeting so tell us Chris, baby!"

As part of the morning routine, Chris stepped into the middle of the room and started his meeting. He said that he wanted to welcome some new people on board and I thought nervously, *everyone's going to look at me.*

Sure enough, he called my name and everyone clapped. There was also another couple of people mentioned. I never thought about where the supposed six new people were that should have been selected. It didn't matter though, because I was in and I was going to make a success of this work opportunity.

Chris talked about the power of choices and the fact that all successful people made choices in their life and committed to those choices and that's how they succeeded. He called out the high rollers from the previous week and started handing out cash bonuses.

He enthusiastically explained the weekly bonus structure; "I have over $500 to give out today for extra bonuses earned last week by the merchandisers and trainers. If you did $800 in sales as a merchandiser in a week, you receive a $30 Shoe Bonus, because we wear out a lot of shoes in this business." Everyone laughed at this.

I thought about my brand new shoes getting ruined. He continued, telling us the trainers would receive 2%, 3% or 4% overrides from their team if the team had $2000, $3000 or $4000 in gross sales for the week.

Everyone had to come up to the front of the room and say a quick word about what they did to earn their bonuses. We were constantly clapping and cheering, high-fiving with each other and backslapping. Everyone joined in, smiling and genuinely enjoying the praise, attention and bonus money.

Chris mentioned that on Wednesday night there would be a pre-management meeting and all the new people would be required to attend. The topics would include the "business opportunity" and how we could grow in the business and where the bigger money was made. I couldn't wait to find out more about the business.

When the meeting was over, everyone started to scatter. Some people ran down the steps and out the door while others milled around. The trainers went to Chris's section behind the partition. Steve asked me to wait in the back of the office until he came and got me.

I noticed that Debbie was busy with the

observations, giving them forms to fill in and Sue was giving the latecomers some merchandise, five to ten boxes of pens to carry out for the day.

Suddenly, it struck me that I was going to have to go out there and sell pens. I was feeling a bit scared and I started doubting whether I could do this. However, it was too late for me to back out now. Steve must have noticed my reticence and immediately told me not to worry, that I would be out with him for the day and he would help me to learn the business and get started properly.

I thought briefly about my final interview with Chris and how he had asked me if I could manage people. Everyone seemed so confident and so far ahead of me. Who was I to think I could be a manager? It hit me that I couldn't tell any of these sales guys how to do anything unless I could do it myself. In addition, I soon discovered that I had other challenges to contend with.

CHAPTER 6 LEARNING POINTS:

LIFE and BUSINESS WISDOM

Where there's people there's politics – Unless you plan on being a career politician it's best to avoid playing the game altogether.

Always pay attention to dress code and be sure to match it but also take it up at least one notch. Better to be classy than trashy.

Your office atmosphere sets the general mood and pace for the day. In sales offices anything that gets staff to come out of their comfort zone is a great start. Singing, dancing, laughing, cheering and lots of fast movement. Whatever you do – do it with passion, speed and confidence and your people will follow.

Pay attention to all your new team members and make sure you help them to feel at ease and include them as active members. Assume they will be a success and they will strive harder to realize your expectations.

CHAPTER 7

Overcoming fear and learning how to sell

Steve asked Chris not to give him anyone else to train so he could focus on me for the day. I was so relieved. I sincerely hoped not to embarrass myself in front of anyone else that day.

Once again, on the way to the sales territory, we had a chance to talk. I felt comfortable enough with Steve to tell him what Zoran had said to me in the lobby that morning. Steve shrugged it off. "Don't worry about that guy. He's not even a trainer yet," he said.

Business Lesson 10

Solid, honest and open relationships are the hidden glue that holds a thriving business together.

I liked Steve's style and charisma. He didn't seem to be interested in anything except building his business. He told me that his goal was to open his own office in Melbourne within the next thirteen weeks. I was blown away at how quickly he was planning on accomplishing that goal.

We pulled up, parked, and Steve got out of the small station wagon and opened the hatch. He started grabbing his boxes of pens and splitting them up into two bags. He also had a couple of small brown rectangular boxes that I hadn't seen before and it was obvious that he didn't want me to see what was in them. One bag was for me and one was for him. He handed me the one without the mysterious items in it. "You ready to roll?"

"Yup, let's do it!" I responded.

Steve explained that I should follow him into a few shops and that he wanted to show me a few sales before I began. I agreed. We started by going from shop to shop. Unlike my observation day where we pitched in an industrial area, this was a retail street. Steve explained that he wanted to show me how to work in the retail sector so I would be well rounded and would know how to do both retail and industrial selling to prepare me for when I was on my own. This sounded fine to me.

He said we would move fast, pop into shops that weren't too busy and take a mental note to come back to those that were. This way we could create momentum and not be waiting on other people to finish their conversations. When we approached a grocery store, I assumed Steve would just pass by it. He didn't. He walked right in and started walking up and down the aisles looking for grocery staff. He finally ran across a young shelf stacker placing some cans on the shelf.

"Hey mate, check these out," Steve said, placing the pens directly in the guy's hands. The guy stared at Steve. "I'm from a wholesaler," Steve continued, "and we're moving these pens at way less than half price. How many could you use? Most people are grabbing a dozen. Could you use a dozen?" He asks again not really letting the guy breathe.

Finally, the young man gathers his composure and says, "No thanks. I'm not interested."

I had already turned to walk away when I heard Steve say, "No worries, mate. Have a look at these. They're normally fifty-five dollars in the retailers." Meanwhile he grabbed the mysterious rectangular box out of his bag and pointed at the number, "55", printed on the top right corner of the box. The number had a circle around it and no dollar sign markings, which looked a bit peculiar if you had the chance to think about it. Steve never gave the poor guy a chance to think.

He opened the box slowly and revealed three narrow dress belts with two buckles, one gold and one silver. Steve said, "These belts are genuine leather." He pointed at the lettering on the bottom left of the box. "What's so great about these belts is they're reversible." He slowly folded back the three belts to reveal that the dark brown, dark blue and black belts reversed to light brown, grey and maroon respectively, on the flip side.

Steve placed the box of belts directly in the guy's hands and you could see that his resistance was starting to fade. *My goodness there's some interest in this fellow,* I marveled.

Business Lesson 11

90% of a sale is possession – if you sell a physical product your goal must always be to somehow get the product into the customer's hands.

Steve said that most people were grabbing at least

three boxes, one for themselves and two more to give to friends and family. He also mentioned that he could give them to him for far less than half price.

"Well, how much for just one set?"

Steve responded that he normally didn't just sell one set but if the guy was serious he supposed he could let one go for just twenty-five bucks. Would the new customer like to pay in cash or with a cheque?

"I don't have any money on me," the guy answered, asking if Steve could come back later.

Steve said he'd love to but that he was really busy all afternoon and had some big drops to make later in the afternoon. Steve suggested that he could borrow the money from one of his colleagues at the store.

"No, I haven't been working here very long and don't know anyone well enough to ask.

"No worries. What's your name anyway, mate?" Steve said.

"Pete."

By this time, I was convinced that Steve was wasting his time with this fellow. The guy was clearly just being polite and not really that interested but this only seemed to spur Steve on. He then said something that shocked me. He asked Pete when he got paid. Was it this Thursday? (Thursday is the usual payday in Australia.) Steve's former accountancy experience kicked in.

"Yeah, this Thursday."

"Why don't you ask your boss to front you the money and then you can pay him back when you get your pay?" he asked. "Where's your boss now?"

Pete pointed down about three aisles.

Steve commanded, "Go ask him."

Pete looked a bit apprehensive and very uncomfortable but was already too far into the conversation to say "no" so he started walking over to his boss.

Now Steve did something even more amazing. Obviously assuming that Pete would take this opportunity either to rat us out and get us kicked out of the grocery store or ask his boss in a way that wouldn't approve his small loan, Steve waited until Pete started speaking to his boss then yelled across the aisles. "Hey, mate. Can you do Pete a quick favor? He needs a loan of twenty-five bucks until Thursday payday. Can you front him the cash until then?"

The store manager stared at us for an uncomfortable amount of time, obviously weighing up the situation and then said something that shocked me even further. "Sure. No worries." He then proceeded to pull out his wallet and gave Pete the twenty-five dollars, which Pete then gave to Steve. Done deal.

I was amazed. Steve told Pete that he'd made an excellent purchase and had saved thirty dollars off the retail price for the belts. I assumed to reduce any buyers remorse Pete might have experienced at least until we cleared the store.

After we walked away, I mentioned to Steve that I didn't think that Pete was really all that interested in the belts and that he probably wouldn't have bought them if Steve hadn't persisted and kind of forced him into it.

Steve thought for a minute and said, "Yeah, sometimes I can be a bit too pushy but he's got a great set of belts now."

Steve smiled, and I learned the power of persistent persuasion and creative suggestions, how to turn a "no" into a "yes", and that it's possible to sell to people who really aren't that interested in buying.

Business Lesson 12

Persistence beats resistance every time.

It's time for me to do my first pitch.

After shadowing Steve for a while, the time for me to make my first attempt was growing nearer. Steve had already mentioned when we started the day that I would watch him make a few sales and then I could do some pitching. By the end of the day I would be pitching and selling on my own.

Watching someone else perform and actually doing it on your own are two completely different things. It wasn't as if I hadn't pitched someone for business before. I wasn't that green. When I was eight years old I had gone door-to-door, selling vegetable seeds in order to buy a new bike.

I had pitched people for landscaping and lawn-mowing work during my last year of high school in order to earn enough money to travel to Europe after graduation. I had pitched business owners to paint or freshen up the lines on their parking lots in order to pay my way through university and to travel during my Christmas breaks. And I had just gone door-to-door selling artwork to make enough money to cover my living expenses.

Maybe it was because this job opportunity seemed so important to me in my current situation or because I had sold myself to Steve and Chris and they showed such high expectations for me in their company, I was really starting to doubt myself.

Business Lesson 13

Mind your mental garden; ruthlessly weed out the seeds of doubt, as they accomplish nothing except to steal your personal power. (Okay, enough of the gardening references.)

As we approached the next shop on the high street Steve turned to me and said, "Are you ready to give it a go?"

"Sure, I'm ready," I answered with trepidation. Steve asked me if I wanted to do it alone or have him come in with me for support in case I needed it.

I said I would go it alone. I pushed through the front door and a little bell rang. I could see no one in the shop. Taking a quick look around, I thought, *great there's nobody here so I've got a great excuse not to do my pitch.* I was about to turn and head out the door when a voice from the back of the store called out.

"Hi, can I help you?" I stirred up all my courage as the gentleman approached. I stared him straight in the eye and uttered…nothing. I had completely frozen up. I couldn't speak; I couldn't move. It felt like my brain had zero oxygen and all the blood in my body had dropped to my legs but I couldn't even move them. I couldn't move forward and I couldn't move backwards.

Finally, my body made my decision and my legs started to move as I swiftly turned around and headed towards the door. My only words were, "Never mind."

The guy must have thought I was some kind of nut. Who was this mute standing there in a blue suit looking like he's just seen a ghost?

As I stepped out of the shop, Steve gave me a bewildered look and asked me how it went. I just stood there saying nothing. I couldn't believe what had just transpired. I never would have guessed that I would freeze up like that. Surely I could have just said something, anything to break the ice and get the conversation going. I was really disappointed in my poor performance.

Steve tried to get a word out of me. "What did the guy say to you? Was he rude?" I just looked at Steve and put my hand up to signal him to stop probing.

I felt as if I had been in a near death situation. I had fled. All my sports training, all my dad's advice – go in hard and you won't get hurt – all my accomplishments thus far in life seemed to have failed me. I realized that I had attempted to go in as an experienced professional salesman but I didn't have clue what I was going to say or how I was going to say it. I'd felt like I was pretending to be someone I was not. It was then that I realized I just needed to go in and tell the truth, to be myself, to show vulnerability and to see if I could connect with this man. He wasn't my adversary. He was just a guy running a shop and maybe he could use some pens.

I made a decision. I was going back in. I looked at Steve without saying a word, turned and walked back into the shop. I found the owner sitting behind a desk in the back of the shop. As I approached, he looked up with surprise in his eyes.

"I'm sorry that I bothered you," I began. "You see it's my first day on the job and I really don't have a clue what I'm doing."

He smiled and responded with grace. "Relax, mate. I was wondering what was wrong with you. So tell me what you're doing here."

That was my cue to approach and show him my pens. My pitch was awful – no structure, no building of impulse. I just showed the pens and explained that we were importers and we're marketing these pens for wholesale prices. He said, "Thanks but no thanks." He encouraged me to keep going and said that he was sure I could find some interested customers further down the road.

This was a turning point for me. I realized that I could pitch people with an honest story, my story, and they would respond in kind. I was proud of myself for walking back into the shop. It would have been easy for me to quit or to tell Steve a lie that the guy was not interested and try to move on to the next shop. But something inside of me told me that I needed to go back in and face this guy, the guy in front of whom I had just completely embarrassed myself. If I was going to succeed in life I needed to fight my own battles and do things on my own terms.

When I explained to Steve what had happened, he just laughed. "Well done, mate. You've broken the ice. Believe me it gets easier from here. Shall I go in with you on the next one?"

"No," I said, "let me do a few more then you can go with me and give me some tips."

So during the next couple of hours I honed my pitch.

The Five Steps To A Sale:

1) Initiate - Break the Ice, Smile, make eye contact and show enthusiasm.

2) Involve - Get your product into the customer's hands and explain why you're calling on them.

3) Promote – Stress the deal i.e. 50% off retail prices.

4) Ask – How would you like to pay? Will that be cash or check?

5) Double up – Double your cash. This is your chance to up-sell and possibly sell other products or more of your existing one. (Extra for friends and family while the great deal is still on.)

Steve always stressed that if I was going to be successful at this I must follow the five steps "to a T" and as I started to pay more attention to his pitch I could see that he was pitching in this exact sequence. The best thing about it was that this structure really worked.

I was getting more and more confident and following this pitch process the best I could. My Initiation (first contact) was getting better and it was getting easier and easier to get the product in the customers hand (Step 2) I also noticed that if I didn't build any connection in my introduction then people generally weren't receptive when I tried to get them to write their signature or something with the pen. This was a really important step for building impulse before attempting to close the sale.

Business Lesson 14

A chain will always break at its weakest link.

I was learning the importance of process. I was now actively involved with the process of selling and learning how to build an impulse in the customer. With each customer, I was getting further than the previous one but just couldn't seem to close the sale and take the money. Thankfully, Steve was patient with me and worked with me for the rest of the day.

I could get the customer just about to the point of sale then Steve would jump in and close it off for me. Like any great leader he encouraged me and gave me all the credit for each sale. I knew differently, of course, but was really enjoying the work and the learning curve I had undertaken.

Up to this stage in my life nobody had ever taken the time to explain to me the selling process. This was truly an eye-opening experience. I was learning and applying all in the same day. I was getting more and more excited about this business. Steve was an amazing role model for me. We were having a blast. We were having fun and making money.

"If you are open minded and easy to teach I can train you. If you are close minded and hard to teach then why should I invest my time teaching you?"
Stephen N. Adgemis

CHAPTER 7 LEARNING POINTS:

LIFE and BUSINESS WISDOM

Smart leaders invest time and money in their people to ensure they get the proper training, coaching and mentoring to succeed in their careers.

You have to manage your fear and treat it as a motivator to spur you on and not as a de-motivator to stop you from moving forward. All success or failure is determined by how well you manage your fear.

All successful businesses work with tried and proven systems and ensure all their staff and contractors follow the system.

Practice makes permanent. In every worthwhile endeavor there are no short cuts to success.

CHAPTER 8

Going Solo

I didn't get much sleep the night before my first day selling on my own as my adrenaline and imagination were on high alert. I was in the office early and completely pumped to get out there. I was a bit shy and also weary of talking to guys like Zoran so I thought if I acted like I was busy organizing my merchandise then nobody would bother me until Steve came out of his Trainers Meeting. Then I would have someone to talk to. As I was finishing the "merch-up" morning ritual, and slowly organizing my pens and my ration of four belt sets securely in my merch bag, I felt a tap on my shoulder. It was another very super confident, happy and charismatic gentleman.

"Hi, my name's Jeff. Are you the new guy on Steve's crew?"

"Yes," I began but before I could finish my sentence he interrupted.

"Steve's a great guy. You're lucky to be on his team. He really knows the business well. Hey, have you seen my goals? Come over here and have a look." On the wall beside the big white board was a huge goal sheet made up of three huge orange poster boards taped together. They were covered with lots of pictures and writing. It took up the entire space from the ceiling to the floor. The pictures were magazine cut outs of beautiful girls in bikinis, sailboats, motorboats, fancy cars, mansions and a map of the Gold Coast.

"Here," he said, pointing to Brisbane on a map. "I'll be here in thirteen weeks."

"Wow," I said. "Really?"

"Yeah, I'm just in the process of building my crew. I've got ten guys already and will be promoted to Assistant Manager within the next few weeks. I'm in a competition with Steve to see who gets promoted first and I'm kicking his butt a the moment." Jeff had an obvious Canadian accent and later told me that he was from Winnipeg, Manitoba. He said he jumped at the chance when he was selected as one of Chris's original team members to come Down Under and expand the company.

I had never met anyone who spoke so confidently and enthusiastically about his goals. Jeff was already having the time of his life, living and working in Sydney, one of the greatest cities in the world. He had set massive goals to make his life even better by opening his own office in Brisbane, situated just north of the world famous beaches of The Gold Coast. At that moment I had the urge to follow him there.

Business Lesson 15

Goals are just goals unless you make them personal. Make them big, wonderful, sexy and alluring. Let them speak to your deepest wants, dreams and desires and you will inevitably attract others to help you on your journey towards their accomplishment.

Things suddenly got busier in the office. Steve came out of his meeting with Chris and saw me talking with Jeff. He thanked Jeff for looking after me and explained that I needed to start practicing my pitch with some people in the office before our crew meeting began.

I agreed, and started with one of the new women in the office. The exercise was a simple role-playing exercise. We alternated between playing the roles of uninterested customer and sales merchandiser. As the customer, the idea was to try to throw each other off by giving excuses why we weren't interested. The salesperson's job was to smoothly give rebuttals and carry on with the pitch, ultimately winning over the customer and making a sale.

We were to keep pitching and giving rebuttals until the customer said "no" in any form at least three times. After three rejections we were allowed to move on to the next potential customer.

This morning pitching ritual was the mandatory default mode in the office. You were reprimanded for taking too long to merch-up in the morning or spending any time with your head buried in what we called, the merch-bag. Clearly, my escape technique had been discovered. These guys were masters of understanding human behavior. In the crew meeting, Steve welcomed some new people onto his team, and praised me for making my first sales on my re-train.

This was debatable but I wasn't about to point that out. He mentioned the money and sales of a couple other crewmembers then said, "Okay, you see that crew over there?" He pointed toward Jeff's team. "Yeah, they're bigger than we are but they are only quantity. Even though our team is smaller, we're of a higher caliber. Now, let's go mess them up. I want you guys to repeat after me and follow my lead. Shout louder and louder then we'll go surround them and interrupt their team meeting. We're not five. We're not four. We're not three. We're not two," Steve shouted and raised the right finger count into the air. "We're number one! We're number one! Repeat after me."

We keep chanting, clapping in unison, and gesturing the right numbers in the air with our fingers. Then we shouted in his team's faces. Jeff tried to keep speaking but we drowned out his voice. His team stopped listening to his sales lecture and started laughing with us. We got louder and louder until Jeff finally gave up. He shouted, "Losers," while using his thumb and forefinger to make an L on his forehead. His team followed suit and soon we were all screaming at the top of our lungs.

Finally Chris came out from behind his partition in the front of the office and yelled, "Guys, who wants a meeting?"

It's no wonder this company didn't appeal to everyone and many people like my roommate had decided not to come back after the first interview. I, however, was hooked. These guys were excited, motivated, professional, goal-oriented, fun, ambitious, and just a little bit crazy. *What's not to like*, I thought

This was my kind of company. I had never known a business like this existed. I had never been informed about this kind of company in my business classes. All my economics professors talked about were big corporations. I was asked to read books like "In search of excellence," by Thomas J. Peters & Robert H. Waterman Jr. and "Good To Great," by Jim Collins.

I had been educated to believe that my future would be in some large corporation made up of serious business people doing serious things. Yet here was a bunch of young guys running a business that was all about learning, growing and having fun in the process.

After the meeting, I literally ran out the door. I noticed that, like on my observation day, most of the team headed to the sandwich bar across the street. I could hear Steve's voice echoing in my head. "Those guys are more excited about getting a breakfast and making that sandwich bar rich then getting a jump on their day and making themselves successful."

I jumped in my car and headed to the only territory I knew how to get to quickly, Maroubra Junction. It was just down the street from my current residence and there were tons of shops. I was sure that nobody had discovered it yet. My plan was to get a jump on everyone and sell out quickly.

I parked my car and got out my merch bag. Pens still there – check. Four boxes of belt sets – check. Pen in front shirt pocket for easy reach and placement into unsuspecting customers hands – check. Build up my nerve – check.

Dom, I said to myself, *why are you wasting your time? You have already done all this and you already know the merch is set properly and everything is prepared and ready to go. Now we're only waiting for you to get into gear and start pitching, so GO!*

As I headed to the first retail door, I noticed a piece

of notebook paper taped on the outside of the front door that read in handwritten ink, "NO PEN SALESMAN ALLOWED". *This is not a good sign.* My lower brain, which I'll refer to as Mr. Reptile, is saying, *go! Run! Get out now! DANGER AHEAD!*

I sheepishly opened the door and stepped in. I say hello with a big smile on my face. "I'm just in the area from a wholesa…" I began. The guy immediately interrupted my pitch and pushed his hand out in front of his chest, motioning me to stop what I'm saying. "If you're selling pens you can get the %$* out!" he said.

I knew I should have listened to him but my enthusiasm is urging me on. I thought I would skip a few doors and then try a more unassuming approach. A few doors down, I went in and started my pitch. "Hi, how are you?" Big smile, make eye contact and exude lots of enthusiasm. "I'm just in the area from a wholesale company." *She's all ears,* I thought. *No interruptions so far so keep going.* "We're doing a test market in the area and I would like to show you a few samples of our merchandise and get your opinion on it."

Smooth, I thought. She looks intrigued and keeps looking at me while she's styling her customer's hair. I looked at the customer and said, "She's doing an excellent job. You're gonna love it when you see it." She laughed. *I can't believe how cheesy I am.*

I reach into my breast pocket and start to pull out my wonderful pen. "Ohh," she groans, "not pens. We get so many of you guys in here. Don't you have anything else but pens?"

"I sure do," I replied. "We have these excellent belt

sets today, too. They sell in the shops at fifty-five dollars but we're selling them today for just twenty-five bucks."

Darn, I thought, *I'm not supposed to say the word "selling" in my pitch, but "letting go" or "moving" but not "selling." Get your act together, Dom?* I could almost hear Steve's voice saying, "Don't ever drop your pants immediately or your price."

"No thanks. You should probably go to another place because nobody in this area would be interested in buying pens, belts or anything else you might have."

"No problem," I said. "Thanks and have a nice day."

I pitched a few more shops and got basically the same responses: Not interested. Oh no! Not you guys again. We've got plenty of pens. Can't you read the sign on the door? I've got pens coming out my ears.

I have no clue how to deal with this, I thought. *Maybe they're right and I should go to another area.* I can remember Steve telling me that I should stick to my area. It was one of the seven steps to success – never leave your area. Yes, I thought, but what about an area where everybody has seen the product? And nobody's interested. I took their advice and ignored Steve's. I got back in my car and drove about twenty minutes down the road to what I thought was a remote set of shops just off Maroubra Highway. I parked my car and grabbed my merch bag and spent a little less time preparing myself.

Into the first door and BAM! the same excuses. Someone's already beat me to the punch. *Where can I go?* I thought. *Where nobody's ever seen these pens?*

Then the negative thoughts began. *This is not easy; in fact this business is really hard. I can't do this. Nobody could do this. I need to think hard. Where can I go where nobody's seen this merchandise?*

I was really feeling down and defeated and then I heard the echo of Steve's voice in my head. *Mate, there are seven steps to success in this business and as long as you follow them you will be successful.*

> **Step 1:** Have and Maintain a Positive Mental Attitude. (PMA= OPM positive mental attitude = other people's money.)
>
> **Step 2:** Be Professional. Dress well, be on time, keep your appointments. (If you're not early, you're late.)
>
> **Step 3:** Be Organized. (Know your who, what, where, when, how and why.)
>
> **Step 4:** Stick to your area. (Don't skip your territory. Hit every Business.)
>
> **Step 5:** Be Persistent. (Keep working as long as it takes to hit your goal.)
>
> **Step 6:** Take Charge. (Take charge of your actions, your selling process and your daily targets.)
>
> **Step 7:** Have Goals. (Think Big – Act Big. Selling the merchandise is important but even more important is your goals to get your own office.)

I recalled Chris mentioning in his morning meeting that the system never fails but people fail to work the system. I ran through each of the seven steps to success in my mind and realized that I was not following them at all. I was skipping businesses and territory, losing my attitude, hadn't yet worked for eight hours. I was losing sight of my goals and wasn't taking charge. And to add insult to injury, there was an office challenge I had to contend with. The "high roller" or top salesperson of the day would get the opportunity to smash a "pie-in-the-eye" of the lowest roller of the day. It appeared at this stage in the day that I was the top candidate. I couldn't bear to think about my embarrassment if this were to happen. *I must figure out a way to sell something, anything. How can I keep from embarrassing myself? And don't forget you still have to figure out how to earn some money.* I was torturing myself with my thoughts.

I made the same decision as the previous time when I had frozen in front of my first customer. I needed to confront my fear and make a new outcome. I decided to drive back to my original chosen territory and get back to work the way I'm supposed to – follow the system. I was going to pitch every door and take more control of my customer interactions. I would stop thinking small and consequently pitching small. I was not going to give up, considering that I had not even been able to follow the simplest of instructions. *I can't blame the system if I don't at least try to work the system and give it a fighting chance to work for me,* I thought, encouraging myself.

I looked back on my first two days with Steve and remembered that he had received some of the same excuses from prospects that I had but had just kept plugging on. He always maintained a positive attitude and pitched at the same level of intensity right to the end of the day, even when it looked bleak and he wasn't selling anything. I remembered his big sale at the end of our first day together in the field. *Of course, this is possible,* I

80

thought. *It's not that it can't be done. I need to sell myself first and then offer my products. Me first - products second. I can do this.*

I got in my car and sped back to my original territory. *Maroubra Junction, here we come again. I know you've seen the pens but you haven't truly seen me yet. Here I come again with more power and resilience than the first go around.*

I parked my car and grabbed my bag and was off with revived and determined energy. Everything was going well until I approached my fourth doorway and noticed that the man sitting behind the desk had what looked like one of our pens. *I don't want to bother him*, I thought.

As I was backing out of his door he looked up and said, "Hey, mate, what ya doing? You're not selling pens are ya?"

Just as I was about to say, "No, you must be mistaken," I decided to play it out instead. "Oh this is great. I see you have one of our pens already."

"Yeah," he replied, "and I've got a problem with it. The guy who sold it to me said that it was real gold-plated. Come over here. I want to show you something." The guy was frowning and sounded pretty annoyed. He was pointing at the tip of his pen and demanded that I come closer. This was not looking good and I was trying to keep some distance when he said, "Here, come closer. You gotta see this." He pointed purposely at the pen tip, which was no longer gold. "Plus, look at this. The black is wearing off, too. These pens are no good and I don't appreciate the way your company lies to people."

I'm searching my brain for a way out of this. "I'm

81

really sorry," I began. "It's not our policy to lie about our merchandise. These pens are meant to be sold as a kind of replica of the Cross pen. Why do you think they're going so cheaply? I mean, if you were to buy something similar to this in the retail shops they would go for over thirty dollars. I have a gold-plated Cross pen set that my uncle gave me for my university graduation and my mom said it probably cost him over $100.00 for that set." I'm trying everything in my arsenal to sell myself and try to calm this guy down. I didn't know the company's policy with complaints and wasn't sure how I was supposed to handle this situation.

Then the disgruntled customer said something that really threw me.

"Have you got a few more of these on hand? If you do I'll take five more off you."

I was dumbfounded but I didn't want him to change his mind. "Sure I do," I said. "That'll be twenty-five dollars. Will that be cash or cheque?" He gave me the cash and I was out the door.

Wow, I thought, *I can sell to people who are disgruntled customers and, even better, I can sell to people who have already bought the product.* It didn't matter if someone had already been through the territory. Clearly, some of the people who work in the company were making up lies to sell more. Steve never sold that way; in fact, I can remember people telling him the pens were crap. Steve just responded, "Yeah, they are but at least we're selling it for half price."

I was pumped and carried on the rest of the day selling what I could and ended up making about forty dollars my first day. By the end of the day, I was mentally, physically and emotionally exhausted. I was upset that I hadn't sold any belt sets and felt like I had cheated the company because I skipped territories. This had obviously cost me selling time.

When I entered the office and walked up to the top of the steps, Chris was standing there ready to greet me.

"How was your day, Dom? Did you have some fun and make yourself some money?

"Yes, but I don't think I did that well. I only sold about thirty pens altogether and no belt sets. I could have done better."

"Forty bucks! Wow! That's great for your first day on your own!" He stuck up his hand for a high five.

He made me feel so great about my first day's accomplishments that my energy was starting to come back. He went on to tell me about the pre-management meeting being held the following evening and explained that he would go into more details about the management side of the business there.

Oh right, I thought. *After such a demanding day there's still a lot more to learn in this business about why I wanted to do this in the first place.*

I gave back my unsold merchandise and paid for what I had sold. This was called settle-up. Debbie made a big deal about how great my first day's sales had been and said that I may have qualified for my first day bonus.

"What's that?" I asked.

"Oh, didn't they tell you about it? Well, you'll find out tomorrow in the meeting." *Oh no*, I thought, *more attention.*

I was on my way out of the office when Steve

showed up waving a big wad of cash in the air. As he passed me, he said, "Hey, mate, how was your day?"

Before I could answer, he said, "Hang in a sec," and hurried over to the desk, grabbed two clip boards and a big brass bell, and started ringing the bell like crazy. Chris, Debbie and the few people in the office started clapping and cheering.

"What's with the bell?" I asked Steve.

"Look at this cash, mate. When you do over $300.00 in business you get to ring the bell. I had a massive day and made over $100.00 again today. Now, tell me about your day."

I told him how I had done and that I was upset that I hadn't sold any of the belt sets. Steve asked me to give him a pitch on the belts. I did and when I was finished he said, "Your pitch is fine. Did you Double-up? (Step # 5 of the 5 Step Selling process) everyone you pitched today?"

"Everyone I encountered?" I asked.

"Yeah, everyone." Steve countered.

"I thought we were only supposed to double-up people who bought something from us?"

"No way," Steve answered. "You should Double-up everyone you pitch. If they say "no" to the pens then you grab the pen out of their hands and say, 'No worries. I've got something even better for you. Wait till you see these, you're gonna love em.' If you do that tomorrow, you're guaranteed to sell out before the day is over."

I left the office that night feeling much better about my first day. Chris's positive reaction to my performance and Steve's advice[2] on the importance of Doubling-up every customer I pitch. As well, it appeared that I wasn't the worst performer of the day so I had somehow escaped the much-dreaded "pie-in-the-eye."

---

[2] The term "coaching" was not in the business vernacular at this time in my sales career so I will not use it too often throughout this story. We called in teaching, training, helping or advising.

CHAPTER 8 LEARNING POINTS:

LIFE and BUSINESS WISDOM

Make sure your goals are grandiose enough to inspire others into action. Everyone aspires to have more fun and adventure in their business life. If you have a well thought out and motivating plan then you will be surprised how many people will support you and even enlist on your journey.

Pay attention to your personal avoidance tactics and ruthlessly propel yourself towards positive actions.

When a company has a tried and proven plan- you should follow it first with your best energy and passion before deciding it won't work and trying to short cut the system. If you want to prove the system doesn't work you still have to follow it diligently before you can honestly decide it's ineffective.

A positive coaching atmosphere in your office at the end of the day is equally as important as the morning kick-start lessons. The salesperson can sleep on it and absorb the lesson and be fresh to act on it the next day. Most sales offices neglect to utilize this opportune time to develop their people.

CHAPTER 9

Day 3 - "No" doesn't really mean "No"

I went home feeling much better about my day's performance from all the positive feedback I got from my trainer and the office manager. I only had enough energy to grab a quick bite to eat, watch a bit of television, have a quick chat with my roommates and then off to bed. I spent another night pitching in my sleep. My brain was trying to make sense and organize all the business lessons I was exposed to during the past few days.

I was looking forward to applying some of the sales tips Steve had given me. It was exciting to have made a bit of cash to start paying some of my bills. If I could just make enough to pay my monthly expenses then I knew I would be on my way to success.

When the morning meeting started, I had forgotten that I might be getting a bonus. Chris mentioned that there were a few cash bonuses he wanted to hand out and that some new guys in the business were already setting a great example. He invited them to come up to the front of the room and give a quick speech.

Oh, no! I thought, *I can't get up in front of all these people and say anything.* I had already frozen up in front of a customer, now I was going to have to stand in front of the whole office. I was scared and my thoughts started spinning. I had memories of all those terrible speeches I made at school and university – those times where I couldn't escape my turn to get up in front of the class. This was one of my biggest fears and I was adept at avoiding it. I never volunteered to go first in class just to get it over with. I would sit quietly and hope that time would run out before it was my turn to speak. I had skipped a few classes at times to avoid the inevitable. Over the years, I had even been able to convince quite a few of my teachers to allow me to hand in a written report in place of speaking in front of the class.

I was starting to shrink and my head was feeling light.

"So, this guy did an amazing job yesterday," I heard Chris say. "He went out there on his first day on his own and made over fifty bucks for himself." *Whew*, I thought. *I only made forty, so he couldn't be talking about me, could he? Oh no! He is. He's just exaggerating my performance to motivate the crowd. Oh no, what will I say?*

"And Dom, come on up to the front and grab your bonus."

I crept out from behind the crowd and headed for the front of the room.

"So, Dom, congratulations!" Chris said. Tell us how you did it!" He looked at the crowd. "Do you guys want to know how he did it?"

"Yeah," everyone in the office yelled. "We want to know! We want to know! Oooohhhh, we all want to know so tell us, Dom, baby!"

All eyes were on me. Somehow I managed a smile as I looked at the crowd and said, "Pitch 'em high, look 'em in the eye and watch them buy!" Mentally thanking Dr. Seuss and all those years of reading his books, I ran back to my spot in the semi-circle and breathed a sigh of relief. Everyone gave me high fives and patted me on the back.

At the end of the meeting, Chris mentioned that there would be a pre-management meeting that evening starting around 7:30 p.m. and to make sure we have a great day, hit our goals, get back and de-merch in time for the meeting.

"If you have any family or friends who would like to know more about the business and the opportunities, they are free to come to the meeting as well," he added.

Once again, as I passed by the take away bar, I noticed even more merchandisers and trainers crossing the street to go grab a bite to eat before leaving for the territory. *I'm getting a jump on everyone today*, I thought.

I drove out to my territory and started pitching right away. I was applying every single thing I had learned thus far and was hitting every door, unless the shop was too busy with people. I knew it was important to pitch retail employees who weren't very busy. I learned how easy it was to lose a possible sale if a customer walked through the door when I was in the middle of my pitch. It only took a split second for the potential customer to lose their impulse to buy.

Building up the impulse was essential to the close. Once the impulse was built and the customer seemed interested then we were instructed to close. We could always go back to the presentation and stress the deal if the customer didn't respond but so often they responded with a question like, "How much are they again?" or "No thanks, not today," or, "No money."

Other excuses included, "I just work here. I'm not the manager or owner."

Our office impact that morning was all about how to deal with negatives. We were taught to always agree with the customer, no matter what they say and then turn the negatives into a positive. Some typical negative responses and our creative rebuttals went like this…

"No money."

"No worries. Most of our customers who don't have cash are either borrowing it because they don't want to miss out on these great deals or are paying by cheque. Do you have your chequebook with you?"

"I'm busy."

"Yeah, me too. I'm busy with all my customers today that are so happy they saved so much money on these great bargains. That's why I said I would just take a few minutes of your valuable time. What are you busy doing today? Maybe we should change places. You do my job and I'll take over yours." This would be followed up with a big smile.

"Not interested."

"Yeah, I know you're not interesting. I'm sorry I can't help you with that but what I can do is give you a great deal on these pens."

"Your products are crap."

"Yeah, but at least it's crap at half price. Can you believe they charge full price for this crap in the shops?"

I know it is hard to believe that we could be so cheeky, bordering on sarcasm and get away with it. But this was part of the fun of the job. We were taught how to have fun with the prospects and still make sales. Now, very few of the people we approached turned into paying customers with these cheeky responses and not everyone appreciated the slightly sarcastic approach. But it's amazing how many people chuckled at the cheekiness and loosened up a bit. This alone spurred me on to talk to the next potential buyer. It was this way of fearlessly approaching people of all classes and all walks of life that was so appealing and so much fun.

I didn't feel stuck in my job. I could go in and out of all these places where other people were stuck working. If the boss of the warehouse was an idiot and treated me badly, it didn't matter. Half the time I had already made a few sales to his employees before I pitched him anyway. I enjoyed feeling empowered working for myself. Just the fact that I could go in and out of all these different businesses and connect with so many different types of people and see all these different professions was educational and fun enough for me.

I was highly motivated and my quick in-and-out approach was helping me to find more and more customers. It seemed that I would hit people just at the right time. I was selling to people sitting at bus stops, people working in factories, retail assistants, and office workers sitting behind desks. The key was not to pre-judge anyone. Just pitch them with the same passion and enthusiasm regardless of what my pre-conceived thoughts were telling me. I learned very quickly that you couldn't tell 100% whether or not people were interested in your products. You just had to give everyone a great pitch and go from there.

Once I got over the fear of pitching to any and everyone I encountered. I realized all they could do was to say, "yes or no". My fieldwork philosophy was all about having fun talking to people and making money in the process.

My tactic was to ignore all my personal inhibitions and judgments. For instance, under normal circumstances I would look at a business like a lawyer's office or doctor's office and pitch differently by mere virtue of the serious and controlling atmosphere these types of offices project. But if I didn't look at the sign before I walked in then I wouldn't tense up or treat them differently than anybody else. I pitched every place with the exact same high enthusiasm. Obviously, I could tell if my form of enthusiasm was appreciated or not. I found that if I just plowed on, oblivious to my customer's apparent disapproval, I could somehow win a smidgeon of their human side over.

I could often times flip them out of their serious state to a more playful state.[3]

I'm not saying I sold in these places because of this tactic but I can say for sure that they didn't slow me down and I didn't skip their businesses because of their exclusive natures, and on those occasions when I did make a sale it was always a big one.

"Do you have an appointment?" This was a common question in offices.

---

[3] Little did I know at the time I was proving "The Reversal Theory" developed by Dr. Ken Smith and Dr. Michael Apter. I was flipping people from Serious (Telic) state to Playful (Peretelic) state.

"No, I did have a lot of phone calls from companies in your area though, who asked me to drop by and show my products. Were you one of the companies that called?" Replying this way usually gave me just enough time to get my pen out and into their hands before they even had time to realize I was just barging in and having fun.

Business Lesson 16

People are people. If you're bold enough to break through their protective professional exterior they will often take a break and join your fun.

I created a few philosophies that allowed me to be bolder than my polite education would have allowed. People often complained about how much they hated their work and how boring their jobs were. These complaints were my philosophical fuel when I barged into their offices to show my products. "Hi Everyone," I would shout as I interrupted their work, "it's time to stop working, take a small break and do something fun like a bit of shopping."

"Our attitude towards others determines their attitude towards us" *Earl Nightingale*

By the end of the day I had sold all four of my allotted belt sets at twenty-five dollars a set plus another thirty pens. I was exhausted and exhilarated. By Wednesday, it looked like I had already made enough to pay my rent and a portion of my grocery bill. My goal of surviving and thriving away from home was starting to take shape.

CHAPTER 9 LEARNING POINTS:

LIFE and BUSINESS WISDOM

A great pitch builds massive impulse (internal motivation) in the prospect by connecting with their needs, wants and desires. But without a strategic close and system for handling rebuttals the impulse will surely die along with the potential sale.

There is no substitute for consistent and sustained trial and error in the field.

Creating and maintaining personal work philosophies is extremely important to keep you on the right path. Laser-like focus on attaining work mastery will ensure your continued success.

CHAPTER 10

What's in a meeting? The three-hour presentation that altered the course of my life

I had no clue what to expect from the scheduled pre-management meeting. I could never have predicted how a simple business plan would take over and dominate my young adult life. I was about to embark on a 10-year journey that would take me around the world building businesses in 11 different countries and lead me to some amazing personal experiences.

Chris, a young "hotshot" of a businessman had an extremely personable presentation style. He encouraged, inspired and captivated many of the attendees including me with the company growth plan and the possibilities for building our own businesses within the companies organization. I was lured in bit by bit as he spoke about people who had already reached their goals by following this plan. Not only did Chris show us a path to building our own teams, incorporating our own businesses and setting up our own offices but also a system whereby we could keep growing by helping others achieve the same thing. We could reach the top and help others to reach the top too.

He reversed the saying, "It's lonely at the top." He explained his vision of how it was actually going to be quite "crowded at the top" when we hit our goals. We didn't have to feel guilty about going for it because there was plenty of room for everyone.

This concept rubbed against my classic economic education. My studies were focused on a world where resources were limited; all economic activity was about supply and demand. Success was tied to your organizations ability to keep your ideas hidden from the outside world. Companies like Coca-Cola achieved greatness because they kept their formula hidden from everyone including their own staff.

The way Chris explained things; there was potentially enough opportunity for everyone. All we had to do was follow the business plan and accomplish each level and once we had reached a new level, our job was to help others to achieve the same. This in turn would propel us even higher.

The better we could do, the better our crew could do. It was all about creating a "people helping people" business. These were concepts and ideas that I had never been exposed to. The first time I heard them, they spoke directly to my core values as a human being.

My Catholic upbringing was also being challenged. I felt that I was a good person and should not be made to feel guilty for having ambitious goals, especially if I helped others to achieve their goals and ambitions. How amazing was this? I thought. This was exactly what I was looking for. I felt so lucky to have stumbled upon this great opportunity. If I hadn't given my roommate a lift for the interview that day then I would never have investigated this possibility.

In hindsight, I would have probably answered one of

our company's ads in the newspaper as they were running every week, but who knows? Maybe, I would have jumped on a plane to go to Hawaii or Denver, Colorado because my money reserves were dwindling. That was my equally attractive Plan B.

As with the closing of a sale, the timing in my life to find a great opportunity was perfect. I was sold.

My plan was to work hard and get promoted to the position of trainer. I would build my team to a strong ten to fifteen people then get promoted to assistant manager. I would get my office training and then go open an office back in my own country. I wanted to open Charleston, South Carolina. From there I would expand my organization across the USA and become a company Vice-President. All I had to do was to help eleven other people to get their own offices and I would be promoted to the position of Vice-President.

I understood that I could make money by running my own office. I could also be selected to run a specific division and earn a commission off every sale. As well, I could earn overrides/commissions off every office owner I personally promoted to run their own business. I was so blown away by this concept of growth that I immediately made a plan that would allow me to hit my goals and retire, financially independent, before I was thirty years old.

Why Charleston South Carolina? I had great memories from my family visits through that city and vacationing at nearby Kiawah Island. It was a highly motivating thought for me to imagine that I could set up my own business and live near the beach.

Until now, I'd had no idea if I would be able to live and thrive outside the USA. My brain was stimulated and my goals were starting to crystallize in my mind. My emotions were stirring and my imagination was on overdrive.

I drove home that evening practically on fire. *I can't wait for the morning to get out there and ring that bell*, I kept thinking.

If I rang the bell three times in one week I could be promoted to a trainer's position whereby I could start building my own team and work towards becoming a manager. What appealed to me most about the meeting was the certainty. If I achieved this then I could get that. Chris wrote the whole plan on the white board and presented "The Big Picture" in such a way that it felt achievable. If we were willing to follow the system and put in the hard work then any of us could make our dreams come true.

"This business is a meritocracy," Chris explained in his meeting. "You don't have to be a graduate from a prestigious university. You don't have to come from a wealthy family or have well-connected parents. All you have to do is work hard and keep learning the business. Once you prove that you can sell and teach others how to do the same, the sky is the limit."

I didn't have to sell my soul to a big corporation and be a "yes man", I proudly thought.

CHAPTER 10 LEARNING POINTS:

LIFE and BUSINESS WISDOM

If you can create a well thought out and compelling plan that includes higher and higher levels of learning, earning, growth, awards and prestige, people will gravitate towards it and work hard to achieve the top spots.

The only limits you have are those that you put upon yourself, so think big to be big.

Never underestimate the power of appealing to people's financial dreams and always make sure you're honest about the hard work involved to achieve such success.

CHAPTER 11

My Third Day Re-train – Learning Valuable Lessons

My head was spinning all night so that I could barely sleep. I felt ecstatic. I could envision my plan to become successful. All I needed to do was to keep improving my sales skills and performance then learn to teach and transfer those skills to others. Before long, I could build my own crew and get my own office.

I was now consistently the first one up every morning in our house. That meant that I was the one also responsible for waking the cockroaches. Our Maroubra house was infested with them. We set off a pesticide bomb every two or three weeks to try to get rid of them but we were all young and too busy with our lives to deal with them, and it cost too much for us to hire an exterminator. So we just learned to live with them. The problem was that these things were huge and we had hundreds, if not thousands, of them.

They would scatter and disappear out of plain sight when you disrupted them. The first place they congregated was in the shower. When I entered the bathroom in the morning and flipped on the light, I could watch them scurry into the cracks and down the drain. I know it seems gross and creepy but there were so many that we used to joke that we had become one with them. The next encounter with them each morning was in the kitchen. I would open the cabinet to get the cereal where it seemed they were waiting on me to wake them up so they could scatter out of sight.

This was not my ideal living situation but it was all I could afford and my flat mates were great. As I said earlier, I only had an air mattress to sleep on and even it had a slow leak in it. For work clothes I had only two dress shirts plus my blue suit and one other pair of dress pants. It was really hot and I desperately needed a few more shirts and maybe another pair of business slacks to get me through the week.

On Saturdays, I understood, we could dress casually. They called it Saturday cruise and Chris was already promoting how much fun it was going to be and how much money we could make when we went out in teams.

The thing I really missed though was my music. I was an avid music fan and had travelled with quite a few cassette tapes and CDs. My boom box had been stolen along with my gold Seiko watch Gamma (my grandmother) had given me. When I first arrived, I had stayed for a week in a really dodgy youth hostel in Surry Hills, in downtown Sydney. One day while I was out and about in the city, one of my six roommates decided to check out and take my watch and boom box with him.

When travelling, you quickly learn the art of non-attachment. Losing belongings to theft is one of the many setbacks that can occur when you're on your own on the road. If it's not hidden away and locked down then it will probably be gone when you need it. What hurt me most is the sentimental value my watch held. I cherished my Gamma and was shocked and disappointed

101

that someone had the audacity to go through my suitcase and take out the most important possession I had. I was deeply hurt and searched the hostel up and down, even threatening a group of Maoris who lived there semi–permanently. They were bemused but at the same time, a little cautious of me while I rifled through their stuff looking for my personal possessions. They could sense my rage and must have felt a bit sorry for me because they ended up inviting me to spend the rest of the afternoon at Coogee beach. This helped to calm me down a bit and gather some perspective.

Having gone through experiences like that I now fully appreciated my newfound ability to make some daily cash in order to cover my basic needs. I began to set some goals to make life sweeter. While pitching in Maroubra Junction, I had caught a glimpse of a boom box selling for about two hundred and fifty dollars. I immediately set my sights to start saving for this baby so I could get music back into my life again.

When I reached the office on day three, Steve informed me I would be working with him for half the day. He would be helping me to get my sales and earnings to the next level. He said he could help me make the same amount of sales he was making if not more. He mentioned it was just a matter of working on my pitch and my work rate. I was skeptical because I thought Steve was a master and that I could never do what he did. I didn't have the self-confidence he had and I couldn't imagine myself assuming the sale as effective as he could.

Nevertheless, it was good to see him back in action.

Steve was again with a few more new people (Observations) and another new agent that Jeff had hired.

When I asked him why he was training Jeff's team member, he explained that he and Jeff helped each other out by training each other's people. Jeff had a different style of pitching but was equally capable of ringing the bell. He did Jeff a favor by helping his people to get stronger and better at the sales and Jeff helped his team to do the same.

"Everyone wins if they work with each other's people, applying the same passion and intensity that you would train your own team," Steve pointed out.

Business Lesson 17

Create your own mastermind group of trusted colleagues and leverage each other's strengths.

I knew Jeff would be great to learn from and work with. I had already been exposed to his motivational and fun style of working when he ran over his amazing "Gold Coast" goal sheet.

This time around it was a different ball game, Steve's pace seemed much slower than usual. I had assumed he would start pitching immediately and that we would follow his lead but today he seemed to be acting a bit funny, not like himself at all. I wondered if there was something wrong with him.

He was taking his time getting all his stuff out of the car and seemed to be almost apprehensive about getting started.

I thought, *well, maybe his strategy is to let us hang out by the car and get to know each other before we get started.* But that didn't make sense. Steve liked to get out there and pitch straight away. He's a guy that doesn't even stop for lunch when he's going for his daily goals.

"Steve," I said, "what are we waiting on? Shouldn't we get going and start making some headway?"

"Good idea," he said. "I was wondering when you would be ready. I was just waiting on you guys. You go first."

He said that the best way for him to help me get better was to watch my pitch for about ten doors then he would give me some pointers.

"By the way," he said, "do you always take this long to get started pitching when you reach the territory?"

"No," I stated. "I was just waiting on you."

"Why would you do that? You're running your own business. You decide when to open and when to close. Don't let anyone but you dictate the pace of your day and ultimately your success."

Another lesson learned. This guy was surprising me and challenging me to learn and grow. I loved it.

At first, I was nervous having these other people walk into a business with me and watch me but I realized that the nervousness faded once I started engaging with the customers. I went in and out of about ten shops. Steve taught me how to introduce my entourage by making a joke once we all marched in and stood there staring at the one sales assistant behind the counter.

"Hi. How are you today? As you can see I brought

some help with me today," I would say. "This is my accountant. This is my banker and this is my boss." The prospect would smile, laugh or comment.

An interesting thing would happen immediately after the initial exchange. It was as if the rest of the troops were hidden or forgotten. The customer focused directly on what I was saying and engaged with me as if oblivious to the rest of their surroundings – unless something happened to interrupt our sales dance. That's why timing is so important. If a random customer walked into the shop, a phone call, a strange movement or a comment by your entourage didn't interrupt you then you could precede through the five steps and have a decent chance of getting a sale.

This phenomenon doesn't happen only in direct selling. It occurs in all one-on-one communication and exchanges. If there's an interruption to the back and forth of real communication then the impulse gets lost. You might as well stop what you're doing and go to the next potential opportunity because it's extremely difficult to recapture the rapport once it's been broken.

This kind of thing happens all the time. There is no need to cry over spilt milk. Among other things, life is about interruptions and missed opportunities. The great thing about my business is that I could simply move on to the next shop and try again.

As it turned out, Steve identified quite a few bad habits I had already developed. This was after only two days of working on my own! This is the importance of the third day re-train, as we called it. After two days that a new recruit had been on their own, a trainer was required to go out with their team member, no matter how well they were performing. This was a two-fold exercise that both reinforced good selling habits and skills and rectified bad habits. Using this method, the bad habits didn't have a chance to get too engrained and potentially ruin a merchandiser's career.

It emphasized the difference between training someone who had just started out and was doing okay on their own, and someone who by making small adjustments could end up becoming a huge asset to your team. Someone "new" could go on to be a top trainer and maybe even a manager on your team one day rather than just an average sales person. Sometimes only small changes were required for someone to get inspired enough and start performing well enough to become a trainer. Without such help the average sales person might get discouraged, slowly decline over time and in the end probably just give up and quit.

Steve caught my bad habits just in time. First, he showed me how slowly I walked between doors. He said he could have pitched five businesses in the time it took me to pitch one. Second, I was using the words "buy" and "sell". I learned never to use these words when speaking with a potential customer. It psychologically focuses his or her attention on spending money, which you don't want because nobody wants to be reminded about the fact that they're about to spend "their" money. Use the words, picking up or grabbing when talking about people purchasing your product. Replace the word "selling" with "clearing out" or "letting go". This connotes positive actions, which appeals to people's imaginations.

We think in pictures. When you mention that the lady just around the corner just grabbed a dozen off me not only for herself but to give to friends and family as a gift, the new potential customer actually paints a picture in her mind's eye. She actually creates her own vision of the event. When I pointed out to Steve my uncertainty about using this tactic he just smiled and looked at me as if to say, "Poor guy. He's suffering from honesty in marketing syndrome." Then he said something that really changed my perspective.

"Look Dom, I know it seems like you're telling fibs and I can see how you would feel uncomfortable pitching in this way but you have to see it from the customer's perspective. They really want to buy but they need to be convinced that ...

1) It's a good deal. They're even happier if they can get a better deal than everyone else.

2) They are not being swindled. By explaining that other people are "grabbing them up today by the dozen" it builds trust and "social proof" that it's okay to buy because others have already bought.

3) They can be happy using the product for themselves or to give as a nice gift.

"How many people were in the office this morning for the meeting?" he asked.

"About twenty," I answered.

"Don't you think that out of all the merchandisers out in the field right now, at least one of them has sold a dozen pens to a customer?"

"Sure," I said "Maybe."

"We sold over 1000 pens in the office yesterday so

107

you could potentially use that as your reference and say to the customer that our pens are in such high demand that we're moving over 1000 per day, then ask how the customer would like to take advantage of this great promotion before we run out. You can say, 'I looked in the warehouse this morning and noticed we only had a couple of thousand left, so would you like to grab our last thousand pens before their gone?'"

That's it! I thought. *I'm looking at this the wrong way. I'm selling based on my own small reality and not seeing the whole and truthful, bigger-picture, larger-living reality beyond my own little sales business.* My pitch was forever altered that day and I shared this amazing insight with every merchandiser I trained from then on.

The other big lesson of the day was that Steve said I was wasting time with people who weren't buyers. Thus I wasn't able to see enough people to hit my goals. He shared a strategy whereby I could quickly glance at my watch and look back at the customer with a sort of grimace and say, "I hate to be rude but I've got a fixed appointment up the road that I really need to attend, so…do you want to grab some pens real quick while I'm here because I really have to get going?"

This tactic worked great as it immediately and surprisingly focused the customer on the action of buying thus they would inadvertently give you their real reason for not wanting to buy. You could easily work from there or in some cases they would surprise me by saying, "Sure, give me a couple then."

He taught me all of these lessons by observing my pitch in only about ten doors. That was it. The re-train was over. Steve needed to get going to make his money for the day, as well as, train up his observations and first day guy. I needed to take his lessons and get busy putting them into practice. I wanted to make up for all the time we spent, or should I say, invested, to develop my selling skills. This training time was essential if I were to succeed in my new profession.

Business Lesson 18

> Always put the necessary time and proper training into your new people on your crew. They are like sponges and will soak up all your good habits and bad habits.

The day ended well. I was able to make my consistent sixty dollars and ring the merchandiser's bell. Steve came back missing the two observations and towing a very enthusiastic re-train with him. He rang the office bell and flashed over $150.00 in profit in my face.

How does this guy consistently make over $100.00 every day? I thought. *I've got to learn exactly what he's doing and beat him at it one day.*

CHAPTER 11 LEARNING POINTS:

LIFE and BUSINESS WISDOM

Great marketing involves using the truth and expanding it to appeal to the customers' imagination.

Train your team until they've got it. Don't assume they've got the right working methods just because they're getting great sales results.

Never use the words "buy, sell, or interested" in your sales conversation. Replace them with action words that create thought pictures, like "grabbing, moving, and love."

CHAPTER 12

Day 4 – Hit more Businesses

By now, I was getting conditioned. My energy was high; I could keep my attitude positive for most of the day. I understood how to create impulse and appeal to both the logical and emotional facets of human response in order to build enough want and need to close the sales.

Today was going to be an unbelievable day.

New Merchandise arrived! *This is going to be a massive day,* I thought. We received in a whole new shipment of calculators. The belt sets, which were already sold out was a great second product to show in case people either bought the pens or weren't interested (remember Step #5 Double-up – to Double your cash?). Now, I was able to offer another product to my customers: A small grey, unsophisticated, indestructible, desktop calculator.

Lifetime guarantee, Chris had told us in the meeting. "Look they're indestructible," he confirmed as he skipped one across the meeting room floor. "We're going to be moving these today at twenty bucks and you guys will be making four dollars a pop. If you can see three hundred people today and sell to ten percent of those, you will have at least thirty customers. Double-up the calculator to only a third of those customers and you've already put forty dollars in your pocket. Move

111

another four dozen pens at five bucks a piece will net you over $60.00 bucks at roughly $1.30 profit per pen and you've got over $100 bucks for the day. Who's excited about that?"

"We are!"

"So, let's sing a song before we go!"

"Ahdi -ahdi- ahdi -oh!" He shouts with all his might.

"Ahdi -ahdi- ahdi -oh!" The crowd follows with a roar.

"To the top we will go!"

"To the Top we will go!"

"I don't care what people say!" he yells.

"I don't care what people say!"

"I'm gonna make $100 today!" Steve yells.

I'm gonna make $100 today!" we scream back.

We shouted and screamed and got our emotions as high as possible. I headed out the door to kick some major butt. *One step closer to getting promoted to a trainer,* I thought. One step closer to making enough to buy my boom box, one step closer to becoming successful and getting my own office.

As I was sprinting out the door another merchandiser on his way out intercepted me, "Hey man, how are you? Can you give me a lift out to my territory?"

I tried to pretend I didn't hear him and my initial gut reaction was to say "no". My polite parental and societal conditioning led me to say, "Oh, I don't know. Where do you want me to drop you off?"

"Oh, I dunno. I don't want to take you out of your way. Where were you going to go?" I didn't want to tell him but said I was thinking about heading to Rosewood.

112

"Oh, I know that area," he said. "It's big enough for the both of us. Why don't we work it together? It should be fun."

I really didn't want to do it, not because I didn't like the guy or had any thing against working with someone. Rather, I was really enjoying my solitude. I liked to drive out to the area on my own, work at my own pace and take breaks when I wanted. I was my own supervisor and I loved it. Now this guy wants to work together? Aaargghhhh!

"Okay, I guess so," I said half-heartedly.

As I was pulling up to park the car I had eyed a store where I wanted to begin my day. It just looked like a place where I could have some good luck. By the time I parked and we got out of the car this guy said, "Al right, I'll start on this side of the street and you can do the other side." He headed straight for my store I wanted. Within minutes, before I was even able to get to my first business he rushed out with a huge smile on his face yelling, "Hey mate, I just dropped a dozen pens in there and one calculator. Great start to the day."

"Congratulations." I grimaced as I headed to my first door.

Needless to say, it was a very tough day for me. I was upset at myself for caving in, for being too nice. This guy didn't have a car and probably wouldn't have been able to get here easily with public transport. Also, I hadn't taken control and claimed the side of the street I wanted to work.

Customers were not wowed or impressed by my "new calculators". They already had their own and didn't need another one. Of course, everyone had already seen the pens and had pens coming out their ears. Even my standard office rebuttal, "Wow, that must be painful," seemed to fall on deaf ears. (Pardon the pun.)

Nevertheless, my day was doomed before it began because I went against my gut. I didn't do what I knew was right. I didn't follow the seven steps to success. I lost my attitude; I didn't take charge, and I hadn't work my territory correctly. The day was a total disaster.

I struggled through and only made about fifty bucks. The ever-illusive $100.00 was getting farther and farther away.

When I got back to the office that night I vowed to myself that I would stand strong and not let people so easily take advantage of me. There were certain people in the office whose methods weren't conducive for my long-term success. This guy was one of them.

When I told Steve about my day, I started giving him my excuses as to why my performance was slipping and how I'd probably made a mistake starting my day by giving this (not so poor) guy a lift and allowing him to share my area. I complained that I couldn't figure out why so few people were interested in our new products?

Steve was not impressed and wasn't about to let me off the hook that easily. "Look," he said, "I had three people with me today and still pulled out $130.00. So that's no excuse. I thought you wanted to get promoted to trainer? How are you going to do that if you're losing your positive attitude and letting other people affect your day?"

"Did you work the law of averages?" he demanded.

"Sure," I replied.

"How many people did you see today? Did you see three hundred people like we talked about in the meeting this morning?"

"Yeah, I must have seen closer to 500 people," I countered.

"How do you know?" Steve asked. "Did you count them?"

"Well, no, but it seems like I..."

Steve stopped me and said, "Look, the law of averages is not a joke, it's a science! It won't work if you only see 150 people or even 200 people. Do you remember studying the Law of Large numbers in statistics class?"

"Yeah, kind of," I said.

"Well then, you'll remember that there generally needs to be a certain number in the sample before it works consistently. Much like when you flip a coin, you know statistically that you have a fifty-fifty chance of getting heads or tails but how many times do you have to flip it before the fifty percent can consistently be proven? Fifty flips? A hundred flips?"

"Yeah, I get your point, Steve," I said.

"I don't think you do," he countered. "If you did, we wouldn't be having this conversation and you would be making a hundred dollars a day like me and you would be much further ahead in the business. You might even have been promoted by now!"

Wow, this guy is really bearing down on me. I thought, *just when I need a bit of understanding after this tough day even my own trainer is giving me a hard time.*

My personal pity party only lasted a couple of moments before Steve spoke up.

"Look," he said, "I suggest you come in tomorrow and go out there and actually count how many people you're seeing. Just scribble on a piece of paper or something. The magic for our business kicks in at three hundred people. Right around that mark you'll see that 10% sales starts to kick in – consistently."

Who's to argue with my classically trained accountant Leader? I reasoned. I decided to get home, get some rest and come back with a vengeance tomorrow.

Business Lesson 19

When coaching and training people, give them the strong advice they need to succeed, not what they want to hear.

"And Dom...one more thing," Steve added. "Remember, it's not the merchandise you're selling; it's you. Have you noticed that some people in the office sold out of the calculators and others struggled to move even one?"

"Yeah, I noticed."

"Why do you think that is?"

"I guess some of us just thought because it was new and exciting to us that it would be the same for the customer," I responded.

"Exactly! And remember it doesn't matter what you're selling. What matters are you, your attitude and your enthusiasm about what you're doing. Sell yourself first, always, before you show your product or service.

Otherwise, you'll always be fighting an uphill battle."

Another great point, I thought. *I have so much more to learn.*

There was a saying we always used to use in the business that holds true for all coaches, teachers and parents. "People don't care how much you know until they know how much you care." This is corny but true. I knew that deep down Steve wanted me to get promoted. He wanted me to succeed and be able to make a hundred dollars a day. I knew I could be an instrumental part of his goal to open his office in Melbourne.

Our promotional system worked like this. You needed to build your own team of people. You had to develop five trainers (three first generation - meaning you directly hired and trained them in the field and two second generation - meaning one or two of your trainers had developed a trainer). Once this team structure was built and maintained you could start calculating your team sales (turnover). You needed to hit $10,000.00 per week two weeks in a row for your "official" promotion to Assistant Manager. Once this title was achieved you were only four to six weeks away from setting up your own office and getting your own business incorporated.

Jeff's team was getting bigger and bigger. Chris was promoting his crew's performance and his total numbers were getting up to the $10,000.00 he needed in gross sales to get promoted to the position of Assistant Manager. He had enough people on his team; he just needed to develop more trainers. He already had his three first generation trainers. All he needed was his two second-generation trainers in place before he could start

117

"officially" counting his sales for the minimum sales required, two weeks in a row, to get his promotion.

I couldn't help but notice that Steve was upset by how quickly Jeff was building his crew in Steve's home country. This charismatic Canadian was tapping into people's hearts and minds faster than Steve. Jeff was showing us all how quickly a person could build a team and hit the criterion for management. The healthy competition raged on.

CHAPTER 12 LEARNING POINTS:

LIFE and BUSINESS WISDOM

All selling relies on the "Law of Averages" know your numbers so you can set your expectations.

Follow your gut instinct and stick to it - in sales and in life.

When coaching and training others it's important to push them hard to be like you and not give into their excuses, reasons and explanations of why something can't be done.

Always focus your efforts on selling yourself first before presenting your product or service.

CHAPTER 13

Day 5 – Keeping the Drive Alive!

I had a good night's sleep, mainly because I was so knackered from the day before. I couldn't even remember if I was pitching in my sleep like the previous nights. This was a good thing because my mind was rested and ready to receive more positive input.

I got to the office and Steve was ready to get us all pitching and learning more so we could all perform better. The office vibe was split with regard to the inclusion of the calculators to our sales inventory. Some loved them because they had sold out the previous day and the others were feeling a bit down because they hardly sold any.

Steve asked me to give him a pitch in front of the crew meeting. I hated this activity. Fear of public speaking coupled with the fact that I was supposed to be good at this pitching stuff by now meant I should be comfortable with speaking in front of a group of people. Steve had been promoting me in his team meetings. Chris had also mentioned in one of his morning meetings that I had been moving fast through the business and he was looking for me to be one of the next trainers.

I was put on the spot and didn't have time to think about being nervous or scared.

"Dom, show us how you pitch the calculators," Steve commanded.

With no time to think, I break into my pitch. "G'day mate, how ya going?" Clearly, I had adjusted to the local slang and pronunciation.

"Not bad. How are you?" he responded.

"I'm just in the area from an import company and we're doing a test market on some new items we just got in. Here, have a look at these," I said as I smoothly slid the calculator into his hands.

"Oh yeah, these look pretty good. How much are these selling for?"

"Well, they normally retail at around forty-five dollars in the shops but because we're wholesaling them in your area today I can let them go for way less than half price. How many were you thinking of?"

I was feeling pretty good about my response. I hadn't dropped my price and I took control by asking a counter question to feel out where the customer was heading.

"Umm, I was only thinking about getting one or two but tell me, what make are these?"

"Oh, I'm not real sure who makes them. We import them and they are similar to Casio. Have you heard of Casio?" I counter. *Everyone must be impressed with my quick thinking,* I thought.

"And does it have any scientific functions? And what about the guarantees?"

I'm trying so hard to answer his questions and do it in a clever way so I can elevate my standing in the group and impress my mentor at the same time.

"Well, it doesn't really have any scientific functions

but it is guaranteed and is practically indestructible. Shall I show you how tough it is?" I reach out to grab the calculator out of the potential customer's hands. This is another ploy to see if the customer is truly attached to the product. If they are, they will want to hold on to it instead of letting it go too easily.

"Oh, that's too bad because I actually needed two scientific calculators for my two sons so they could use it for their school work."

I start to counter and Steve just puts up his hand for me to stop. "Let me stop you there." Turning to the others in the room he said, "Shall we hear from the group how Dom's pitch was?"

I know I went wrong in a few places but I really didn't feel comfortable under everyone's scrutiny. First, Steve asked me what I thought I had done well before he asked the group the same question.

I felt that I had a good introduction. I thought I smiled and showed enthusiasm with my tone of voice. I thought my involvement (Step2) went well because I was able to get the calculator in the customer's hands, since nine-tenths of a sale is giving the prospect a sense of possession.

The group concurred and added that I had good eye contact and seemed to respond well to the customer's questions.

"Now, what about areas where he could improve?" Steve asked.

"Well, I didn't really take charge," I said. "I didn't get a chance to close you and ask for the order plus I didn't know how to respond to the question about scientific functions."

The group backed me up on my improvement points and couldn't come up with any more challenges I was facing. Steve then asked if he could let us know what he thought. We all were eager to hear what the master had to say.

I felt so much more relaxed amongst the group by now and was pleased that they hadn't ripped me apart like I thought they could have. I had shown some vulnerability and they had responded in kind. Steve's coaching style was usually extremely open and supportive and this time was no different. We all learned from each other tips to improve our knowledge and skill at every team meeting.

"Well," Steve said, "in your introduction you asked me how I was and I responded with 'good, and how are you'? Remember?"

"Yeah."

"And then what did you say?"

Ah man, how rude was I? "I said that I was in the area from an importing company."

"Exactly. You weren't listening to the customer at all. Remember you have two ears and one mouth so you should listen twice as much as you talk."

"Yes, Steve. Got it"

"Plus," he continued, "that was your great opportunity to say something like: Man, I'm doing so great. Thanks for asking. I'm so busy filling orders in the area but I thought I'd drop by and let you in on some of the great deals we've got going at the moment."

Wow, this guy's good! I thought.

"The next thing and the biggest thing you could improve on is what?"

The group started throwing out some educated guesses.

"Closing?"

"Pitching bigger."

"Giving more personal space."

"Better body Language."

"No, nope, sorry mates, you're not even close." Steve said with a smirk. "Do you give up?"

We all nodded. "Beyond Dom not getting a chance to close me off, did you notice how much time he wasted answering my questions? In fact," he continued, "I timed him and I noticed I easily wasted two minutes of his time. Now, that may not seem like a lot but add that up over the course of your day. In fact, how many buyers are we looking for each day?" He waited for our mental calculation.

"About thirty," everyone responded. "Ten percent of three hundred."

"Yeah," he says, "and some of you aren't finding those thirty buyers because I know that everyone didn't ring the bell yesterday. I was the only one on the team to make over a hundred dollars. How much time, on average, does it take to make a sale?"

"Three to five minutes," the team answered.

"Okay, if we take four as the average and multiply that by thirty buyers then all our money is made in about a hundred and twenty minutes of your day. If you are wasting two minutes per customer then is it possible that say by the time you've pitched a hundred and fifty people you would have wasted over three hundred minutes of your day. Could it be possible that some of your buyer minutes get wasted with people you're spending time with who just simply aren't interested, who are just wasting your time?"

Man, I thought, *this is so true. I've been wasting time with really nice people who had no interest in buying my product. They just like the interaction and communication but had no interest in buying and probably just liked to talk.*

I'm not sure if Steve's mini-impact session made an impression on anybody else on the team but for me it was a huge learning point. I was on a new mission to count how many people I was pitching during the day. I was going to master the skills and not be excited just because I found someone who would actually take time out of their day to look at what I had to offer.

It wasn't just the negative people I had to be aware of. In fact, after four days I had probably heard about four hundred ways to say "no". I was becoming immune to these negative responses. I also needed to beware of "time wasters", these beautifully nice people that made me feel good by showing interest in me and my products but who had probably zero intention of purchasing anything.

When will the learning stop and the high earning kick in, I wondered. *I'm off to see three hundred people today if it's the last thing I do.*

I found it difficult to keep count as the pace of the day picked up. I would talk to five people then mark it down on my little tally paper. I was moving way too quickly to stop after every pitch and make a tick mark.

I had been pitching for about four hours and felt that my day was half over so felt compelled to count my tally.

125

I took a small break and started calculating my list.

This can't be, I thought.

I recalculated, only seventy people in four hours? This company is crazy. It's physically impossible to see three hundred people a day. Here I was thinking that I must have been pitching closer to five hundred people. Now that I was actually counting, it seemed that a hundred and fifty people a day was more the average.

Maybe they're talking about how many people I actually see throughout my entire day including those that I pass on the road, along the street etc., not just the ones I pitch, I thought. That made more sense based on these numbers. The manager was always talking about seeing three hundred people a day. *The joke is on me. I'm such a sucker to have believed these charlatans,* I thought.

Then it struck me. *What kind of work habits did I have? Could I walk faster between the shops? Could I actually pitch more people in between shops in parked cars, at bus stops?* I had seen Steve do all of this and I did it a bit but not as a normal practice. I would be hesitant and evaluate the situation before diving in. Maybe this was my problem?

I decided to pick up the pace and be relentless, work like a madman for the next few hours. I would really go for it and see what I could do. I pushed my energy up high while my legs and mouth worked over time. Within the next few hours I was able to speak to two hundred and twenty people. And I did it! I had my first one hundred dollar day!

I couldn't wait to get back to the office and grab that bell. Not the merchandiser's bell but the trainer's bell. I had done it. I had cracked the code to direct sales. I had worked the numbers game, not wasted time with people, taken control, and worked eight hours or as long as it took to hit my goals. I had worked the five steps to a sale and kept my attitude protected throughout the day.

When I reached the top of the stairs and I saw the big brass bell sitting on the corner of the desk. I sprinted in and lunged toward the bell, grabbing it stretched out in mid-air and rang it like crazy before I skidded to a stop on my side. I leaped up, still ringing it and ran around the office. The few people who were left in the office that night clapped and smiled and gave me a high five. I was ecstatic.

I had proven to myself that the system worked and had made my first one hundred dollar day in the business. I knew where I had been going wrong all that time and was absolutely certain that I could pick up the pace the next day and reach that three hundred people mark. It was all about hustle and time management.

I was reminded of the impact meeting that morning where Chris had asked us all clinch our fist as hard we could. We did and then he urged us to squeeze harder. We did and then he said, "Now, I want you to squeeze even harder! "As we're all screaming and grunting he said, "Now, I would like to ask you, on which squeeze were you more likely to hit your goals?"

"We often miss opportunity because it is dresses in overalls and looks like work."
Thomas A. Edison

As I drove home that evening and reviewed my day I

felt a subtle tingle of excitement building. I was actually becoming successful and I was on my way to becoming who I always imagined I could be. I was modeling myself after Steve and Chris and the other top performers like Jeff. I couldn't believe my luck and I was counting my blessings.

CHAPTER 13 LEARNING POINTS:

LIFE and BUSINESS WISDOM

As you improve your skills - your awareness of the subtle details improves greatly.

The ability to Listen is an underrated sales skill — those that work hard to improve their listening skills are the ones that thrive.

Keep track of your numbers and work the Law of Averages to a "T" - your wallet will thank you.

PART III

The Art of Teambuilding
Unexpected Life Detour
Testing Self-Belief
Learning to pitch to the big boys
Mentors have mentors, too.

CHAPTER 14

Day Six – The Good = My Promotion | The bad = Facing my Fear of public Speaking

I was feeling great about my previous day's profits. I started dividing my daily takings into separate piles. One was for the weekly expenditures for food, rent, transport etc. The other was for essential life improvements like beer and a boom box. I could visualize my new boom box sitting in the corner of my room and with just a couple of hundred more dollars it would be mine.

I entered the office that morning on fire and ready to make more money. I had managed to brush off the guy who was always looking for someone to give him a lift. He must have found another victim more willing than I. I was relentless in my focus to get out of the office and into my car, straight after the morning meetings. If someone other than Steve or Chris tried to talk to me, I pretended I was in too much of a hurry to get out of the office for my appointments. I just kept walking and said, "Sorry I can't stop. I'm late for my appointment. I'll see you in the office tonight and we can chat." This tactic worked extremely well because I was so committed to it and I never stopped walking while I was talking. If I had to turn and face someone I'd continue to walk backwards as I spoke.

Body language is everything in sales and persuasion.

Studies reveal that body language equates to sixty percent of your influence potential. Your tone of voice is around thirty percent and, oddly enough, the words you speak only amount to about ten percent of your influence. Thus the old cliché, "It's not what you say but how you say it that really counts". I was learning to use my body and tone of voice to measure how effective I could be, not just to create sales in the field but also to manage my personal life. I was learning the ability to influence other people's behavior by altering my own. I learned to adopt new habits of relating to people in order to become more productive and get more of what I wanted and less of what other people wanted from me. Life was getting good.

After I did my quick rounds in the office and grabbed my daily stock, Chris came out of his newly constructed office and asked me to come in and have a quick chat.

This was another thing that was really exciting. Over the last few days not only were we learning new skills and learning to produce income for ourselves, we were also seeing the office transform from a 2,500 square foot open plan with a few temporary partitions to a real office with a reception area, administration office, manager's office, meeting room and an empty office with a desk, managers chair and phone. We didn't know yet who would be using that office but had a sneaking suspicion that it would be available for the first person promoted to the position of assistant manager. Jeff and Steve were currently the prime candidates.

"So," Chris started, "you had a really top day

yesterday. What made the change in your performance?"

"Well, I finally figured out that I wasn't seeing as many people as I should. I thought I was seeing over three hundred people a day but when Steve pointed out that perhaps I should count just to be sure, I realized that I was coming up way short. I think that's why I was only making fifty or sixty dollars a day. So, I really pushed myself in the afternoon and ended up pretty lucky."

"You should give yourself more credit than that," he countered. "You can see now why we keep stressing that everyone follow the system."

"I sure can."

"So, do you mind if I ask you your opinion about what you think the rest of the office should be doing to improve their performance?" Chris asked.

I was really surprised by this question. Who was I to tell him what I thought about improving the office's performance. I had only been there for less than a week and he was already asking me what I thought?

"Well, I'm not so sure that everyone is working as hard as they should. It seems to me that they are a bit slow to get out to their territories and if that's how they start their day then possibly the rest of their day is the same." There was a slight tinge of condemnation in my voice.

"You're probably right," he said. "I think some people want it more than others and my goal is to find the guys and girls who want to go to the next level so I can help them to get there. Then they can train and motivate the rest of the office to raise their standards.

How do you feel about getting to the next level? You know, becoming a trainer like I spoke about in the meeting on Wednesday evening?"

"Great!" I said, without thinking. "I'd love to be a trainer."

"Do you think you could show people how to make a hundred dollars a day like you did yesterday?"

"I'm pretty sure I can. I mean, I know I still have a lot more to learn," I said, trying not to sound too overconfident.

"That's great, because you've hit the criteria to be promoted to a trainer and I would like to promote you this morning in the meeting. Does that sound good to you?"

I could not think fast enough to respond with any of my internal fears and inhibitions.

"Definitely," I said. What I was really thinking was, *Oh, no. Does this mean I have to speak again in front of the group?* Of course, it did, and I immediately felt apprehensive.

"What about running the impact meeting on the topic you just mentioned to me. You know, about how you discovered the power of the law of averages and how important it is to get out to the territory quickly and get to work?"

I'm not prepared, I thought. *How could I ever do that? No I can't, I'll freeze up in front of everyone. It will be worse than my first pitch. I'll have the whole office staring at me.*

"Ahhhmm, I would rather prepare a bit more. Do you mind if I could make some notes and then run the impact either tomorrow or Monday?" I asked.

"Sure," Chris said. "That makes sense, how about if you run the impact meeting on Monday. It would be a great topic for everyone to start off the week."

Whoa! I thought with relief. *I've escaped yet again. But all I've done is delay the inevitable. Dom, you've got to get used to speaking in front of people or you'll never be successful at this. Look at Steve. He runs crew meetings everyday, and impact meetings in front of the whole office two or three times a week. And what about Chris? He's the manager and he runs the morning meetings in front of everyone every single day. It seems obvious that this will be part of your job if you're going to run one of these offices.*

I tried to imagine how I could have an office and not have to do that part of the job but knew it wasn't possible. There was no escaping the truth. If I was going to be successful in this business I had to get over my fear of public speaking.

My ambition was on a crash course with my fears and I had only the weekend to deal with it.

When the morning impact meeting started my head was still spinning. I knew Chris was going to call me up in front of the rest of the office yet again. What was I going to say? How would everyone else feel about it? Some of the people had been in the business longer than I had. What would they think? Would they be jealous and hold a grudge? I couldn't worry about that now. I had to think about what I was going to say.

"This next guy I want to bring up is not only going to tell you how he made over a hundred dollars yesterday but has also hit his criteria by ringing the bell three days in a row. He is getting promoted to trainer this morning.

Everybody put your hands together for Dom Kotarski! Dom, come on up and let us know how you did it!"

Chris gave me a high five and then shook my hand and said, "Congratulations. Just say a few words."

I felt so excited that my confidence started to go up. First I mentioned that I wanted to thank Steve for setting such a good example for me and helping me to understand the importance of following the sales system, especially the part about seeing three hundred people. I reiterated why it was so important to get out there and start counting how many people you were pitching so you could stay on track and hit your goals to ring the bell.

I was shocked to find that not everyone ignored me. My worst nightmares of everyone literally turning their backs on me as I spoke never transpired. In fact, quite the opposite, everyone appeared to be listening and respectful of what I had to say. They were smiling and concentrating on my words. I had temporarily suspended one of my terrors. I knew I hadn't conquered it yet but it was nice to know that my world wasn't going to come crashing down the minute I got up in front of my colleagues to speak.

The words just seem to flow and the next thing I knew I was back with the group listening to Chris's daily motivational speech. He spoke about goals and the importance of working each day towards your next level.

"Keep your head in the clouds in terms of what you want to accomplish and your feet on the ground doing the day-to-day hard work."

"By the way, did anyone notice the extra office? Can

you guess whom it's for? It's for the next promotion to assistant manager. Who's that going to be? We've got a couple of guys doing good work and competing to be the first assistant manager in our Australian organization. Jeff and Steve are neck-and-neck. The race is on." Everyone applauded. "The great thing about this business is that there are no surprises. There will never be any surprise promotions. Unlike other companies, here you know that whatever position someone reaches, it was earned. Everyone starts out in the field and builds their own team. The only way to get ahead in this business is to help other people to get ahead. Isn't that great?" More applause erupted.

"Everyone here has a chance to become a manager and get his or her own office. It just boils down to how much you want it and how hard you're willing to work in order to reach your goals. Life's not fair in some respects. Some people will have to work twice as hard to reach their sales target as others. Maybe someone has some natural talent or a special way of dealing with people. The thing is though, if the person with talent doesn't continue to apply him- or herself and continue to improve or doesn't help others to learn the business and succeed both in the field and in team building then they will get passed by. The person learning and growing and helping others will be the one who gets a personal office. It doesn't mean that the naturally talented person can't get an office, it just means that one person might have to be more determined and work harder than the other. That's what doesn't seem fair. The great thing is, everyone gets a chance to succeed in this business. You just have to work hard and develop your skills. You can do it; we all can do it. So let's go out there and have a great day!"

This type of speech was the first of many we would hear and then communicate in our own ways to our troops. It was obviously designed to get those who were already working hard to work harder, and those who were more talented but a bit lazy to apply themselves more so as to not get passed by. This type of daily motivational and instructional meeting touches everyone's hot buttons or personal motivation points.

After the morning meeting, everyone hurried out of the office except for the trainers. Steve said all the trainers needed to hang back for a trainers meeting. I had no clue what to expect. I was itching to leave and really wanted to get out in the field and start my day. Instead I had to go into Chris's office with the rest of the trainers and wait.

Everybody's getting a jump-start on me in the field, I thought. Having to wait for yet another meeting was torturous.

CHAPTER 14 LEARNING POINTS:

LIFE and BUSINESS WISDOM

Relentless focus is the not often talked about cornerstone of success.

Companies that offer fast, next level promotions to their people in the beginning stages of their sales career, often helps them to retain their staff that might otherwise lose their drive and quit for lack of exciting and realistically achievable new titles or positions.

One manager with passion and enthusiasm towards their people and their company is worth 10 x more that 3-5 mediocre managers.

Having an opportunity growth plan in place gives you massive leverage to motivate your top people. But don't expect more than a small percentage of your team to reach the top levels.

CHAPTER 15

Learning to pass on the skill – a.k.a. The art of replacing yourself

Everyone gathered around the manager's desk as he talked briefly about how the morning went. He explained what we needed to talk about in our team meetings and said that we needed to get our people in earlier so we could work on their pitches. We spoke about how each merchandiser was doing and who would work with whom for the day.

Wow! I thought. *Now I'm privy to even more managerial information. After only five full days I have been promoted to a trainer. Now I have a chance to build my own team and start learning how to manage people.*

Everything was moving so fast but I relished it all. My emotions were on full alert.

"Dom, Steve," Chris yelled. "You guys will be taking out six observations (Trainees) to train today. Wait here in the office while I go get them."

Six people? I thought. *How are we going to train six people?*

I glanced at Steve. He just shook his head and said, "No worries. Just follow my lead and we'll have a great day."

I didn't have much time to think. We were introduced to all six observations. Chris explained that Steve was a top trainer only weeks away from opening his own office in Melbourne, while I was one of the newly promoted trainers who was moving fast through the business and was setting an excellent example for all the new people in the business.

We hustled everyone out of the office and away from the laggards. Steve immediately took control and gave his orientation. He explained how we would be spending the full day together and because it was such a big group we would be splitting up and switching around the team as the day progressed. He fed them the "fear of loss" speech that said; unfortunately everyone won't be able to get hired but we would be doing our utmost to ensure that everyone had a fighting chance. We would show the business properly and educate everyone on the basics so they could perform well on the test and final interview at the end of the day.

We split up into two cars and I followed Steve to our territory for the day. When one of our trainees asked if she could drive her own car and follow us, Steve declined saying that it wasn't necessary. "We can all squeeze in comfortably and it's a good way for everyone to get to know each other a bit better," he added.

Steve later told me the main reason he would never allow anyone to take his or her own car was to prevent losing control of the situation. "Think about it," he said. "As soon as that person gets behind the wheel of their own vehicle, you've lost full control of the trainee. They can decide to leave at any time during the day. Imagine what would have happened if I had let you bring your own car when I trained you? You might have left after a couple of hours and never seen me make my big drop at the end of the day."

Steve had made a good point. This was the beginning of my training on how to take charge, and keep control, of my team. I immediately understood how important it was to keep control of your business through the whole recruiting and training process.

"The new recruit is the one looking for a job, not you," Steve explained. "You've got your sales job plus you've got something even better. You've got an opportunity to build your own business to the size that you want. Most people can only dream about an opportunity like this and you've got both a job and an opportunity. The problem is that people will completely dismiss this type of work at first sight until they get a chance to know you and hear about your goals and ambitions. Once they have a chance to understand both you and the reason your going for the bigger opportunity, your chances that they stick around to either watch, join you for a while, or decide to go for management themselves, increases dramatically. The thing is, you've got to keep them with you long enough for them to get to know you and see that you're serious and really making something happen. That's the reason and the challenge of taking charge of your observations long enough to give them a chance to see it and feel it for themselves."

"If you don't take massive control of yourself and learn to guide your people with the detailed direction you want them to take in your business then your people and your business have a slim chance of growing and experiencing ongoing success."

I was way out of my comfort zone and had no clue

what to say or do but I knew I needed to act confident and show enthusiasm about the job at hand. I had no training manual, only the example that had been set by Steve six days previously.

As it turns out the great example he set was exactly the thing I needed to make the day a success. When we arrived at the territory, we found a place to park the car and gather. Steve got out and split up the group. Two people would go with me and four would accompany him.

"Dom, why don't you take your crew and give them a brief rundown on how the day will go," Steve instructed. "I'll do the same. Then we can split up the territory and start working. We will meet up around 12:00 noon for a quick break and briefing before we continue on with our day."

I was trying to act professional, as if I knew what I was doing. Then it hit me like a flash of lighting. "Don't try to be something you're not. Relax, be yourself, and speak the truth." This was my key to relating to others. This was my clue on how to keep from "freezing up" in front of others.

"Okay, everyone gather round," I said. "Today is my first day as a trainer. I got promoted after only five days in the business so I'm really excited to show you what I've learned in such a short time. Hopefully, some of what I've learned will rub off on you and you'll be able to move up in the business as fast as I have, that is if you get the position and if you aspire to grow as fast as I have.

We're going to show our products to various

businesses in the area and get their opinion on them. If they want to buy a few samples they can. My main objective is to show you guys how the business works and make sure you know the basics so you can pass the test and perform well in the final interview. Please stay close to me when I walk into the business and just smile and act like you're a part of the conversation. I'll do the rest."

Everything I had learned from Steve on my "observation day" was somehow poured in my head already and I was able to spill it out. I had no clue how this was happening but was pleased to be able to talk to my observations without freezing up. I was even a little impressed with myself for a brief moment.

In and out of shops on the high street we ran. I was using the standard introduction and got the customers loosened up a bit with, "We're doing a test market in the area and I thought I'd bring along my banker and accountant just in case you want to make a large transaction." Or, "It's my first day on the job and this is my supervisor and his boss who wanted to come out and check up on me."

Both of these introductions actually got a bit of a smile out of the potential customer but didn't always work in terms of effective sales. I hadn't put too much pressure on myself to perform in front of my two trainees but in the back of my mind I really wanted to get some sales under my belt before I saw Steve at 12:00 noon. I really wanted to beat him in the field and this was just as good a day as any to do so.

One thing I quickly noticed while trying to sell to

144

someone with two observations in tow. It was not easy to keep the customer focused. They seemed uncomfortable with the idea of a small gang of people entering their business. Some had a look in their eyes like we were either trying to shoplift or worse, stage a hold up.

I had to adapt a bit and asked one of my observations to wait outside the shop while I walked in with the other and then swapped after a couple of doors. This worked a bit better and I started selling a few items.

I could quickly see that this was getting boring for the "trainees" and one of them said that it looked pretty easy and asked if he could give it a try. I didn't know how to respond to this so I agreed and gave him a box of pens to carry and try pitching. He didn't want me to watch. I knew how he felt so let him go to try it on his own.

When I offered the other observation a chance to do the same, he declined.

The guy actually made a few sales and seemed really excited. I was feeling good about my training practices and decisions so far. That is, until Steve showed up.

"Hey mate, what's going on?"

"Things are going great. I've got one of our guys already selling and this guy just wants to watch for now but we'll see how things pan out later in the day."

Steve immediately read the situation and stepped in to take control. I noticed that Steve had only two people with him. I was about to find out why.

"Okay guys. Let's have a quick meeting. As you can see, we're missing a few people already. Unfortunately, I didn't think they were suitable for the business so I had to let them go. I've already given them some money for a train fare back home or to the office. It's better that they can spend the rest of the day looking for a job more suited to their skill level."

I could see everyone tense up and they listened more intently to what Steve was saying.

"What we'll do now is split everyone up a bit so you can see different styles of pitching. So now the two that went with me can go with Dom, and you two that were with Dom can come with me."

He then asked my eager trainee who already started selling to give me back the pens and the money for the sales. He said, "It's good that you proved how our sales system works but we aren't interested in just selling a few items to businesses. We're looking for wholesale bulk orders." Steve noted that had he been fully trained he might have been able to sell hundreds if not thousands to the customers who just bought one. "Could you go grab us all a coffee?" He handed my trainee (Mr. Eager) some cash while the rest of us headed back to the car so we could get some more merchandise.

As we were walking, Steve pulled me to the side and said "Mate, I don't normally do this because we should never leave observations on their own but I need to talk to you real quick."

When we were out of earshot with the others, Steve said, "I know this is your first day training people and you won't normally have to train so many at the same time, but this is good experience for you. First of all, you should never let your observer carry your merchandise,

146

under any circumstances. It's your responsibility and you're the one who has earned the right to carry it out on consignment. Not them. Remember, you're the one with the job and the opportunity and they are the ones looking for a job."

I nodded as Steve continued. "You gotta take control and keep control throughout the day. That's why I let go of two observations straight away. I wanted to show the other two that this was a serious business and if they weren't engaged and asking questions then there's no guarantee that they will even last the day with me."

"You're allowed to let people go like that?"

"Sure you are Dom. This is your business and you want to attract people you want to work with, who you can train and mold into the type of team you want."

"Chris won't get upset when you get back to the office?" I asked.

"No way! Chris is my partner in business. He would thank me for not wasting his time with unsuitable candidates."

Wow, I thought, *this is a great way to look at your relationship with the manager of the office.*

"Plus," he said, "the way I look at it, Chris works for me. He does the advertising, the initial interviews and screens the applicants for me. All I have to do is take them out and see if they've got potential to learn and do the business. In this case though, where there's a larger group, you sometimes have to sacrifice one or two of the less engaged candidates immediately if they show any signs of a negative attitude or lack of interest in what's going on. If you don't get rid of them quickly and early

147

then their negative attitude could rub off on the rest of the group and you could lose everyone."

"Okay," I said. "I think I understand what I need to do."

"Also, it's not good for someone to pitch or make sales on their observation for a couple of reasons. First, many people have beginner's luck in sales or might have sold before so they have some experience. If they make sales early on then they think they know enough to get the job and they stop learning and paying attention for the rest of the day. They also want to be paid for their sales. So you've lost control of someone who could have learned the system properly and been an excellent team member for you. Plus they won't have experienced a proper "observation day" so they won't be able to train others very well when or if they become a trainer."

Man, Steve is always thinking ahead, I thought. *Very impressive.*

"Did I let you pitch on your observation day?" he asked. Without waiting for a response he continued, "I knew you had sold door to door before because you told me but I wanted to show you the proper way to work a territory and pitch larger quantities than just one."

"Second, it's all about Step #6 – Take Charge. The minute you allowed him to take your merchandise and start to sell, you lost control. I'm not saying you can't allow someone to pitch but you should make him or her wait a bit. Treat them like a rubber band and hold them back. The more you make them wait the more determined and eager they'll become. Wait until they get the job if you can, and then hold them back even more on their retrain day. Then when you finally let them pitch, they are so motivated and fired up they will go far and do great. Just like pulling a rubber band back to its max before letting it go."

I could see the logic in this.

"The only exception to this rule is if they won't stop badgering you. Then you can maybe just give them one sample and be sure to let them only pitch once and one time only. Walk in with them so it's supervised and you can hear what they're saying; listen for the use of the five-step approach. See how they interact with the customer. The chances are they won't make a sale on the first attempt and you will have some learning points for them to consider. If they're over-confident then you should bring them down just a bit by saying, 'Not bad, but you've clearly got a lot more to learn. So let's continue to watch me for a bit more and I'll let you try it again later this afternoon.' Or, if they seem a bit apprehensive and look to you for advice then you can be more encouraging and say, 'Man, that was a great first pitch, far better than mine on my first try. Let's keep going and I'll show you some more approaches and skills we can help you develop to make your pitch 100%.'"

By this time my over-eager observer was back with the coffees and I realized that Steve had made a few exceptions on this day, like allowing the observers to be by themselves for a couple of minutes so he could have a training session with me, and taking a coffee break.

Steve doesn't even stop for lunch, I thought, *and now we're having a coffee break?* I knew this wasn't normal for Steve and that he was showing me how much he cared about my learning to take time out from making sales to explain to me the "proper way" to train people. I took the lessons to heart and vowed to take more control of my observations for the remainder of the day. Steve had also instructed me to be sure not to let one observation stay outside the door. "Bring them both in with you while you pitch and make sure they are standing close to you so the shopkeeper doesn't have to keep and eye on them. That way, you can get them focused on your pitch and how you build impulse in your customer."

We finished our coffees and split the teams back up. Steve took three observations with him including Mr. Eager and I took the remaining positive young woman.

At this halfway point in the day, I had learned enough about training and just decided to "go for it" for the rest of the afternoon. I explained to the nice woman that I was going to work quickly to see as many people as possible, as my goal was to cover the entire territory before it was time to head back to the office.

I went in and out of businesses and made as many approaches as possible. I felt a bit hampered in my approach but soon noticed that once I had got past the introduction and engaged with the customers they soon forgot about my observer's presence and I could build my pitch the same as when I was on my own, just as Steve had suggested. As I started moving faster and getting my blood pumping, the sales started happening and my confidence rose.

My poor observation was getting a good workout. I didn't realize how well I had trained myself to move quickly between the doors. Now that I had someone in tow, it was obvious that I needed to warn my observations ahead of time before I started the day. They need to be prepared to move quickly. The quick pace was an important part of my work strategy and if people were going to go out with me during the day, they needed to keep up.

CHAPTER 15 LEARNING POINTS:

LIFE and BUSINESS WISDOM

Learn to adapt when dealing with people but never let a "live" coaching lesson slip by without acting on it.

It's paramount that you learn to replace yourself with people that are as good or better than you in various positions. Only then can your business grow beyond you.

People need to follow rules and you must have a structure of Do's and Don'ts for all your companies training processes. Be sure your people adhere to the rules.

CHAPTER 16

Creating and Solidifying the Habits of Success

Being a trainer and team leader brought on dual responsibilities. Firstly, I needed to continue to build my sales skills in order to make enough money to stay in Australia. Secondly, I wanted to teach and train others how to do the same so I could build my own team and get promoted to run my own office.

This was easier said than done because I had no clue how to influence my own team. As I mentioned earlier, you can have the best plans in the world but as soon as you account for the "human factor," things become more complex and it's often back to the drawing board.

It matters deeply how you learn to work and behave in your work. It matters deeply what your work habits are and how you respond to the good and bad events in your business. You have to understand that people will appear to let you down when you need them the most. All the while you're learning the most important lesson of all. It's not what happens to you but your reaction that counts.

Even though people seem to let you down, more often it's themselves they are really letting down. It's important to remember they are on a different journey than you. When people disappoint you, as much as it hurts, you must react with grace. Let them know you're hurt but will get through it. Then you must let it go and move on.

What's important is to keep your honor, vision and goals in front of you. Keep striving for what you want to achieve and set the right habits in order to achieve your goals. It really doesn't matter what other people say or do. What matters are your discipline and your commitment to your higher goals.

Little things, like showing up every day to work even if you don't feel like it, are extremely important. Being professional when others are practically encouraging you not to is essential. Being polite, having manners, being consistent with your positive attitude and demeanor, yet at the same time, not allowing people to give you excuses day in and day out. Fight for what you know is right; stand up for the less capable. Show people how much you care by showing them how to work properly and then hold them accountable to do the same for themselves.

These are the things that encourage success in people's lives. Success is not about luck as I have heard so many less successful people try to point out. Luck only comes when you're committed to change your life for the better.

I'm a firm believer that every individual is presented with certain chances that can turn into true opportunities, which in turn can lead to success. It's your preparedness to take action when these opportunities appear that separates those who eventually make it to the top from those that don't.

My story of successful team building was about to

take off in a big way. I was on a roll, and within the following three weeks I had built a team of five people. I had learned to face my fear of public speaking by forcing myself to ask the manager each day to do an impact meeting in front of the whole office. I was running team meetings everyday as part of my requirement as a crew leader. I was diligently preparing all my training material the night before so I didn't feel nervous when I had to speak.

My belief that people would both turn around and face the other way when I spoke or just ignore me completely weren't realistic fears. People really wanted to know what I had to say when I got up in front of the room. Plus, if I had had a good day and experienced a nice learning moment then I had an obligation to share this information with everyone in hopes that they could learn from it and use it straight away in the field. If they were succeeding then we were all succeeding.

I realized that my fear of failure, or lack of success, was a bigger motivator than my fear of public speaking. Plus my motivation and ambition to have my own office was incentive enough once I realized that there was nowhere to hide. I would not be able to run an office without speaking to my team everyday in a public forum. This was the way the company worked and I could see that this was part of the magic.

We were like sponges soaking up information in the field and then ringing it out on each other back in the office at night, with an added refresher in the morning. We were constantly and consistently reminding everyone in the business about best practices in all aspects of the business.

Even if you weren't interested in improving or moving ahead by becoming a trainer or manager you were getting the right information on a daily basis that you would need in order to do so. You got it by default and the office was always buzzing with upcoming events, new products, advancement opportunities and fun.

We were learning, growing and motivating each other. People were moving up the promotional ladder quickly and merchandise was moving out the door even faster. This was absolutely one of the fastest growing businesses in Sydney at this time.

I was getting into business shape. I was learning to accurately observe where people were going wrong in their pitches. I could see if they were weak on their introductions or didn't have an effective close. I enjoyed coaching and advising team members on improving certain aspects of their pitch techniques. I quickly learned that I also needed to encourage them to want to do better.

This was an amazing discovery for me. I could not have predicted how much of my time would be spent motivating and encouraging people to:

1) Believe more in themselves and their ability to solve issues and face challenges.

2) Be motivated enough to try out new strategies and develop better skills.

3) Show up everyday especially on the day after a small defeat.

Short term, Mid-Term and Long Term goal setting

Goal setting skills became a paramount office theme. It felt powerful to set a goal and hit a goal – daily, weekly and now monthly. I created my own "best earning strategy" based on my personal daily sales target. In order to stay and grow in my current situation I needed to earn a certain minimum amount but I didn't want to "feel" pressurized and force my sales. My minimum daily target strategy allowed me to feel relaxed because it was based on realistic and achievable numbers.

I would not stop until I hit that minimum daily goal of only fifty bucks but my maximum and more "motivational" goal was to hit that one hundred and fifty dollar mark each day. My team's motto was, "$150 a day is the only way!" I taught my team to go for their maximum goals too, because it was even more exciting and motivating than their minimum goal. I reminded them that all businesses needed to "know" their bottom line but keep focused on their higher earning possibilities. "Keep your head in the clouds but your feet on the ground" as Chris would often say. I also stressed the importance of personal resolve, not to quit during the day and never come back to the office without hitting at least their minimum goal.

We calculated our minimum goal amounts by working out our monthly living costs including work related expenses – rent, travel expenses, food, clothing, entertainment and various incidentals. Then to divide this total amount by the number of planned days in the field to arrive at our individual daily break-even points.

157

I made sure to sit down with each of my team members and help them calculate their personal numbers so we could arrive at their minimum daily target and their more inspirational profit goals.

Most of my team was young and just starting out. Some lived at home, some were in a share accommodation situation like me, and others were just student travellers looking to make some money while on their gap year.

My job as team manger was to make sure each member knew both his or her bottom line and earning potential. Once established, I would help them to stay on task and ensure they kept focused enough to achieve their targets. If need be, I would personally give them some of my sales to help them reach their daily and weekly goals. As long as my team hit their goals then ultimately I would hit mine.

Business Lesson 20

The fastest, easiest and most efficient way to accomplish your goals is to help others' hit theirs.

I had already saved enough by my second week in the business to purchase my boom box. What a great feeling it was to be able to accomplish that goal! I had covered my living expenses and was starting to improve my personal circumstances. Being able to do this and look after myself in a foreign country felt great. I was feeling more powerful on each passing day.

I constantly pushed to lead the way for my team. It

was so much fun to learn something new in the morning leaders meeting and then turn around and teach my new guy in the afternoon. Learning and teaching became synonymous. As top trainers and team builders we lead by example, we were proving that if you were willing to work hard to hit your daily sales targets then your weekly and monthly goals would start falling into place.

I learned how powerful it was to get new trainees to fill in their goal sheets within their first few days in the business. I would catch them reading all the amazing goal sheets hanging on the walls in the meeting room. They could see how big some of the trainers were thinking. Each goal sheet had pictures of trendy offices, cool cars, massive mansions, huge yacht's and big bank accounts, as well as, written personal commitments about opening their own offices throughout Australia and then expanding their organizations around rest of the world. Everyone in our office not only thought big about what they could accomplish but believed big too. They understood the magic formula of combining their own hard work and ability (not withstanding their commitment to continue developing their sales and people skills) coupled with the company's support would allow them to make their dreams a reality.

The way I got my team motivated to think big and get committed was simple. I waited until they sat through their first pre-management meeting. This was normally within their first few days in the business. Then I gave them a huge piece of poster board and said, "Go for your life and make sure you think big. Write down all your goals and ambitions, both personally and professionally. Then my job is to help you achieve them."

This was one of the main differences for people coming into our business as opposed to most places of work. Without a doubt, this was the first time anyone had ever spoken to them about their dreams and ambitions; and the first time they were ever shown a precise plan of action they could take in order to accomplish their dreams and goals.

Most importantly, this was undoubtedly the first time they had ever come into an atmosphere that was so positive towards individual and collective achievement. A company that actually had expansion plans big enough to include them in it. A business that not only counted on them to be a big part of their growth but also offered a chance to be personally responsible and profit from that growth. A big part of the company's business plan was their support system, which was set up in order to facilitate massive and quick expansion.

The bigger your goal, the better, was our belief. Everyone encouraged each other to think bigger than they ever had before. And this was the key differentiator – it was okay to think that way. Nobody would put you down; make you feel small or foolish. Even if your goal seemed unrealistic, nobody ever told anybody that it wasn't possible.

If you were willing to work hard and follow our business plan into management, anything was possible. This was an awesome environment. The fact that everyone was so supportive of each other made it all that much more special.

CHAPTER 16 LEARNING POINTS:

LIFE and BUSINESS WISDOM

A true professional strives to put on their best performance even when they don't "feel" like it.

Rewarding people for showing the proper work habits is equally important as praise for the top performers.

Having a career plan for your people whereby they can consistently move to higher and higher levels of earnings and notoriety based on their own performance is the key to consistent and ongoing growth.

Getting people to believe in themselves and their ability to achieve their goals is a full time job that is well worth the effort.

CHAPTER 17

Just When Things Were Going Great

I was making some great new friends. We all had something in common. We wanted our own offices. Harvey was born in London but grew up in Sydney. He wanted to go back to London to open his first office and dominate the English market.

Patrick was a traveller from Sweden. He wanted to go with Jeff to Brisbane then open up in New Zealand, eventually making his way back to Europe. Taras, from Vancouver, Canada, had met Chris in Toronto and got excited about the chance to come over and build his crew in Sydney and open up an office there. The rest of the office was made up of travellers and locals from various backgrounds and diverse skills that were all starting to make goals around growing with the company. Some were more adamant and vocal about becoming a manager and setting up their own offices. Others were just there to make some money and see where it all might lead.

"Repetition is the mother of skill." *Anthony Robbins*

The success I was having had a lot to do with my ability to learn from all the meetings and apply the advice and strategies that were shared. Chris held a trainers' meeting every morning before the merchandisers arrived. Then we had our impact meeting and morning meeting and afterwards another quick trainers' meeting before we headed out for the day. Monday evenings we had about a two-hour meeting after we got back from the field and all the new people had gone home. On Wednesdays we had the pre-management meeting. It was mandatory that all trainers attend so we could be there with our crewmembers. If we didn't have any crewmembers there we could take notes on how the manager ran the meeting.

The pre-management meeting was an excellent motivator because we talked about how to run a business, including costs and how the profits were made in addition to the opportunity to become a business owner. To me this information was extremely inspiring because I could see how profitable the business could be.

The consistent meetings with consistent messages from Chris and the other top team builders were having a positive effect on my motivation and confidence. I could imagine myself reaching the top of this business. I wasn't training a crew I was building an empire. I could hear Chris's voice echoing in my head.

The other exciting part of this routine was our Friday Night Beer night. We worked hard during the week so we played harder on the weekends.

Saturday Cruise was about coffee and doughnuts in the morning. We split up and went out in the field with teams of three. We only worked half a day. We came in around 10:00 a.m. and finished in the early afternoon.

The routine was fun and I never had a dull moment.

I didn't have long-term friends or family to demand any of my time so I was in no rush to get home after work. We had built such camaraderie with each other from our shared fieldwork experiences. Naturally, the stories got bigger and better when we had a few drinks at the pub.

On one particular Saturday night we were all on a high after our great week. I had five people on my crew already and was receiving positive attention from the top leaders and company director. Jeff and Steve were building their teams like crazy.

The local pub was not a great place to hang out for longer than a couple of drinks so we decided to move the party to the Rocks. This is the main party strip in downtown Sydney, where all the action takes place. There are restaurants, bars, night clubs, strip clubs – you name it, it's all located on this one kilometer strip in downtown Sydney.

I thought I would be clever and try to fit as many people in my little car as possible. In the end I think we squeezed nine people in this tiny car including the tall Swede, Patrick, who wanted to squeeze into the trunk. The night was crazy; we were spending all our hard-earned money on drinks and all trying to find a partner for the night.

I finally hit it off with a great girl who asked me if I could drive her home at the end of the evening. *My life is improving by the minute,* I thought. *This is too good to be true. I'm building a business, making new friends, and now I'm going to get lucky. Life is excellent and getting better.*

When I left Tennessee, my girlfriend at the time was not very impressed. Without actually speaking the words, we agreed to split up while I was making this journey overseas. I think we both knew that at this juncture in our lives we each had to go our own way and see what the future brought.

If it's meant to be, well then, I thought, *it would be, just not at this moment in time.* I missed her like crazy when I had some time to contemplate but my life was so busy and moving so quickly that I barely had any time to think about what might be. I was on my way to find success and nothing was going to stop me.

When we got in the car this girl told me she lived in Bankstown and wondered if I could drop her off at her house. This didn't sound too promising, and I wasn't sure where Bankstown was but thought I might be able to get to know her a bit better on the way and set up a second date. Plus, by the time we got out there she might invite me in. Or so I hoped.

No dice. When we reached her house, she gave me a kiss and said 'thanks but no thanks'. I couldn't come in because her grandmother was there, sleeping on the coach and we might wake her.

I tried to persuade her a bit more but she wasn't having it. And neither was I. As I drove back home I can remember thinking, man I'm tired. I wish I were home now. I dozed off a bit and then shook my head, trying to become more alert.

I contemplated pulling over to sleep in the car but made the decision to trudge on. I was heading down the highway at a pretty good pace, around 100 km per hour (60 mph). My last thought was, I wish I were home and lying in my bed.... when BAM! I crashed into a telephone pole in the middle of the carriageway.

It only took what seemed like one second to doze off and my life as I knew it had come to a grinding halt. I had been woken instantly by the crash of my chest to the steering wheel, my head to the top of the car and my knees into the dashboard. *Oh, my head hurts, oh my knee. There's blood everywhere.* Time was standing still now and within what seemed like seconds I could hear a voice, shouting.

"Hey, man, are you all right? You better get out of the car," he screamed while grabbing my shoulder.

The door wouldn't open so he helped me to climb out the window. He gave me a shoulder and walked me, limping, onto the grassy bank on the island in the middle of the motorway.

When I looked at my car I could see it was sideways in the middle of the road. The front left was absolutely crushed. Luckily, I had not hit the pole straight on but on the left side and had clearly catapulted the car off to the right and into the middle of the motorway.

I could tell by the worried look on the gentleman's face that I was in a bad way. Blood was everywhere and I looked at the flesh protruding from a massive laceration on my knee. *Damn,* I thought, *I've ruined my nice pair of Levi's.* My next thought was, *Dom, you really messed up this time, just when things were starting to go your way.* I felt desperately tired and all I want to do is to lie down and just go to sleep.

"Wake Up!" the man kept shouting. "Don't go to sleep! Wait for the ambulance to show up!"

The next thing I remember, the emergency team was

waking me. From this point on, I was going in and out of consciousness. I can vaguely remember the ambulance ride and the emergency team speaking about the cut on my tongue. *Oh boy,* I thought, *will I lose the ability to speak?*

All I could do at this point was to go along for the ride. I had no clue how seriously injured I was and what the consequences of my actions would be. All I knew for sure was that everything that had transpired up to now had halted. I would have to figure out how to get better and go back home. *Dom, you're such an idiot, why didn't you just pull over?* I kept thinking. All I knew for sure it that I had failed miserably. And I had done it in the worst way possible by ignoring my common sense and injuring myself, possibly permanently. All I could think is that at least I had done it to myself and nobody else was involved. How bad would I have felt then? My mistakes were only affecting me and no one else. I could breathe at least one sigh of relief.

Once we arrived at the emergency room, the doctor revived me so I could make a decision. He said, "You've done a pretty good job on yourself. "Which do you want me to sew up first – your head, your tongue or you knee?"

This was my first introduction to the extent of my injuries. *Let's get the worst over with first,* I thought. "Uy ung," I gurgled.

The doctor got it. "Okay, we'll start with your tongue. Don't worry, you'll be able to speak again once the swelling goes down."

After all my stitches I was awoken again so the police could to talk with me. "Well son, you're very lucky to be

167

here," the officer said. "You should have been killed when you hit that pole."

This was when I realized how serious my accident was. *I could have died,* I thought. *I don't want to die. I've got my whole life ahead of me. I haven't even had a chance to go out and make my way in this world yet.*

I couldn't believe how stupid I was. Why didn't I just pull over on the side of the road when I felt tired? My recurring thoughts didn't matter now. What's done was done and now I had to deal with the consequences.

As it turns out I had fractured ribs. I had bitten completely through about a third of my tongue; the top of my scalp had a six-inch cut. My knee was lacerated all the way across the kneecap. This deep cut was the result of my knee crashing into the blunt end of the car ignition key which was poorly positioned on the dashboard just left of the steering column. Within 24 hours, I was released from the emergency care unit fully stitched up, bruised, battered, humbled and thankful to be alive.

Everything was happening so fast. My room-mates were in shock and I hadn't had a chance to tell my parents what had happened. Massive pain hit me within hours of being back in my own room and I felt an unbearable agony in my knee. Luckily, one of my housemates worked at a hospital nearby and she called a cab to bring me to emergency straight away. The doctor on duty said my kneecap had been badly damaged and was now infected. It needed to be operated on immediately.

I asked the surgeon how serious it was and he countered by asking me if I played a lot of sports. When

I replied that I used to he said, "Well, you'll definitely be able to walk again but I'm not so sure about running. We will do the best we can but I can't promise a miracle."

I remember waking up after surgery and feeling tired yet relieved. I had IVs sticking out of my arms and tubes coming out of my knee. The nurses were wonderful and kept coming in to check up on me. I still had no way to let my mom and dad know where I was. It felt very strange not having family nearby and even worse for them not to know what had happened. My mom always had a sixth sense and always seem to know if I was feeling down or facing problems. I wanted to contact them in some way but knew it was not possible. It's hard to imagine now but this was in the late 80s before mobile phones and the internet - so texting, messaging and e-mailing were out of the question. As well, hospitals weren't in the habit of allowing patients to make long distance calls. I made the decision that I would wait until I was released from the hospital before making the dreaded call. I hoped that my mom didn't have any of her senses running over time.

I was told that I would be in the hospital for at least a week. This was a time for me to heal and get better. I couldn't get up and move around like I always had. I was bound to the bed. I was left with only my thoughts and a book fittingly titled, "Good as Gold" by Joseph Heller.

I randomly selected this book out of a small selection on the book cart while I was still drugged on pain medication. It served as my only form of distraction from continually berating myself.

You can be hard on yourself for only so long before

you have to start thinking of positive thoughts of renewal. I began to see my situation as a blessing. I had an opportunity to look over the last few years of my life and realized that I had been taking way too many chances. I was not invincible and there were consequences and limits to what my body could handle.

I had been far too careless with drinking and driving and now this was all the proof I needed to realize how dangerous this was. I looked at some of the big nights out I had had during university and realized that all the trouble and fights I had gotten into were due to drinking.

I was lucky to have survived this accident. I was not invincible. I needed to look at my behavioral weaknesses and make some major changes if I were going to live a successful life.

I was sure that I had lost my current opportunity. I could not possibly go out and make my sales now and I wasn't sure at this stage if I was even going to be able to walk properly. At any rate it would be months before I was healed. I would have to go through the healing process and then take the next flight home.

I started taking into account all that I had learned and began to create my own list of successful habits I would follow if I ever got another chance to build a business. I was going to look at my situation with a good attitude and realized that my life is not so much what happens to me but more about how I will respond to my setbacks. And this was certainly one terrible set back I've gotten myself into. But I had survived this car accident and I knew I would have another shot at success in the future. I thought, I planned, I reflected and I dreamed. I took this time to create my own personal system for sales growth and team success. This new system was born out of my strong commitment to get the most out of my bad situation.

See Framework FIGURE 1:

Figure 1.
Dominic's Sales Growth System Framework

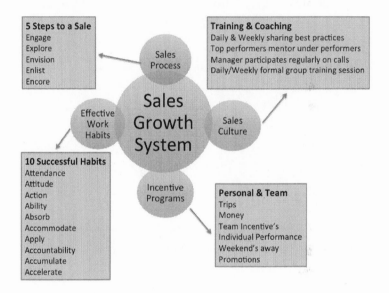

CHAPTER 17 LEARNING POINTS:

LIFE and BUSINESS WISDOM

If you insist on learning from your own mistakes ONLY– you're an idiot.

When you screw up royally – make the decision to take the lesson and move on.

As soon as you think you're indestructible pay close attention because life might show you otherwise.

Accidents can be a lifelong blessing if you treat them as guideposts to learn and grow from.

Never say to yourself that you're unlucky. It's better to say you're lucky and call any unlucky incident just a "fluke."

CHAPTER 18

The Sales Growth System

With so much time on my hands I was able to spend many hours contemplating all my sales successes and failed attempts. I visualized the sales process in my mind and could see how the 5-step process of each sale's pitch melded into the sales conversation with my prospects. I remembered how easy some of my sales were and how others were a constant uphill battle. I thought about how important work habits were to a successful day and came up with various strategies on how I could improve in all of these areas. The system and work habits I came up with for myself and my team were as follows:

5 Essential Steps to a Sale

1) Engage (Introduction) - Go in with high energy and make eye contact, have a big smile and stay with the introduction until you've got engagement with your customer.

2) Explore (Qualification) - Make sure you qualify the customer before you present your product or service. Don't waste your time or theirs. Ask insightful questions. Can they make buying decisions or influence the process? Do they have available funds to make a purchase? Do they have a need or slight desire for your product or service?

3) Envision (Presentation) - Present your product or service and be sure to stress the deal while offering all the great benefits and features.

4) Enlist/Enroll (Confirmation) - It occurred to me that if you do the first three steps correctly then the close really wasn't a huge step at all but more of a confirmation to carry on with an order or to confirm the next steps to be taken.

5) Encore (Maximization) - This was all about maximizing the order. Are there other products that could be useful for them? Do they know anyone else that might be interested? Referrals.

Business Lesson 21

Having a great sales process is only part of a successful sales business; equally as important are the working habits, and guidelines to keep you and your team on track.

Ten Absolute Guidelines for Success

Dominic's effective and fun work habits:

1) Attendance (Show up) – You must have daily discipline.

2) Attitude (Positive Outlook) - The right attitude is necessary to achieve continual success in any endeavor.

3) Action (Work your strategy) - Be pro-active and prepare what tools and resources you need before you start working. The great thing about taking action is that it's 100% in your control. Keep working so the Law of

Averages works for you.

4) Ability (Keep improving your skillset) - Mental tactics, emotional awareness, sales skills, communication skills, technical skills as well as your ability to influence others.

5) Absorb (Sponge it) - Absorb the positives and use them to build on. Absorb the negatives and deflect like a fighter. Maintain your motivation by keeping your thoughts and actions focused towards your goals.

6) Accommodate – Your goals, your customers' wishes and your teams' dreams. Don't forget your family and friends need you too: Maintain balance.

7) Apply – Keep listening, learning and applying your new knowledge; keep focused on applying your business strategies, follow the logical steps and tactics necessary to succeed.

8) Accountability - Take full responsibility for your results, both good and bad. Your power lies within you.

9) Accumulate, Amalgamate and Advocate – Consistently expand and utilize your network – keep making and maintaining business and personal contacts so you can not only stay in business but grow your business. Help others to hit their goals and you will reach yours.

10) Accelerate – Keep focused on moving forward. Teach what you've learned – if you share your new knowledge then you'll be able to keep it and build on it. If you pay it forward it will live on and come back to you in many lucrative ways.

This was my own version of the work habits I swore to follow and maintain if my career was given a second chance. I vowed while my pain subsided and my body healed that I would live a more responsible life in the future. I would respect my body and my health. I wanted to walk again and I dreamed of running. I thought about all the times my coaches had made us run sprints and I use to say how much I hated running. *Imagine if I can never run again like the doctor said.* I felt ashamed of all the thoughts and negative comments I'd made to anyone who would listen. *If I could just get back on my feet and get a chance to run again, I would be forever grateful and thankful.* I could only lie there and pray that this day might come.

"It's getting better all the time."
Line from a Beatles song.

I felt completely alone yet in some ways content. On the one hand, I knew I had made a major mistake and I didn't have any of my family there to comfort me. On the other hand, I knew that I would somehow be able to take some lessons from what I had learned and apply them to the next chapter in my life, whatever or wherever that might be.

I could feel the pain from the operation subsiding and felt like I was slowly healing. The hospital staff was great even if the food wasn't. There was nothing for me to do but lie there until my knee was healed enough to put on a cast.

I was not expecting any visitors because only my roommates knew about my incident so you can imagine my surprise when I heard familiar voices and laughter echoing down the hall. Chris, Steve, Taras, Harvey, and

Patrick had all come to see me.

"How did you guys find me?" I asked with surprise.

"Well, mate," Steve jumped in, "we were all wondering where you were when you didn't show up for our company barbecue on Sunday. It's not like you to miss a get together with free food and grog."

"Oh, God, please don't mention drinks to me," I responded.

"Well, I guess this won't do you much good then?" Harvey grinned as he pulled a can of Victoria Bitter (VB) from behind his back.

"Isn't it illegal to bring alcohol in hospitals?" I said with a huge grin.

I heard Patrick come around the corner with one of the cute nurses in tow. He said in his broken English Swedish accent, "Yes, this is the patient. He needs an immediate sponge bath. He looks horrible!"

She smiled, shied away and said, "I think he's being well looked after."

After all the camaraderie as I told them about my ridiculous story, they all said, "Mate, don't worry. You'll be back on your feet in no time." I told Steve I was really especially sorry because I knew he was going for his sales target soon for his promotion. I wanted to make sure he hit it with all the help from my team. I added, "And by the way, how is my team doing?"

"Aw mate, don't worry. I'm looking after everyone and I'm not worried about my promotion. I'm more interested in you getting better so you can get back in the action."

"Me, too," I said with a bit of uncertainty in my voice.

We continued our banter and laughs and my spirits

were definitely lifted by their visit. On the way out Chris stopped by my bed and said, "Dom, don't worry about a thing. When you get back on your feet come in the office to see me and we'll figure something out."

I couldn't believe it. All hope was not lost, in fact, there appeared a chance that my future had not been completely altered by this major incident. Now I felt even more determined to get better and somehow get back on track towards my successful future.

CHAPTER 18 LEARNING POINTS:

LIFE and BUSINESS WISDOM

Every successful enterprise has a fully functional system or framework for all processes – take the time to develop yours and record the process for you and your staff to follow - Then stick to it

If you do the right thing and treat your team like you would your family through good times and bad then your team will give you more loyalty and hard work than you could ever imagine.

Always give people hope even if you don't know what that hope might be. Life has a way of rewarding people who offer random acts of human kindness.

When someone makes a mistake they immediately pay the price – there's no need to make them "feel" worse by telling them how wrong they were, which inevitably makes them re-live their bad experience. Pain is real and in the now and can be dealt with immediately – suffering is the mental act of beating yourself up for your mistakes and re-living the painful moments – this can be ongoing if left unchecked.

CHAPTER 19

I'm outta here! What's next?

After seven long days I was finally released from the hospital with a huge cast covering nearly my entire leg. I was given instructions to come back in about three weeks to have it removed. At that point if all were healing well I would be put on a rehabilitation program for another eight weeks to build up strength and flexibility again. There was still no indication if I would be able to run again but the doctor was quite stern that I take care and follow all the medical advice. If I did I'd have a pretty good chance that I would get back eighty to ninety percent functionality.

I hauled myself into the cab and the driver asked me where I wanted to go. I said, "Botany Road, Alexandria." I was headed straight to the office. There was no point in going home and staring at the walls in my little room. I wanted to see if there was some way I could help out around the office and maybe learn something in the process.

Chris was just finishing his interviews when I arrived and I asked if I could have a quick meeting with him.

"Sure," he said, "just give me a few minutes to finish up a couple of things." He was on the phone to his supplier in Canada and later to his business advisor, Barry. It turned out that we were all learning the business

180

from someone else. There was helpful advice coming from everywhere.

As I sat in the lobby waiting for Chris to finish his call, I thought about what I would say. I really just wanted to learn more about the business and when I finished my rehabilitation I would head back to America and hopefully be able to get going with something over there. I had heard that the company had offices in America and Canada and thought that maybe there's a chance that I could connect with the organization back there.

Chris was finished with his call. "Dom, how the hell are ya?" he said. "Come on in and tell me what's happening."

"Well, Chris, I just wanted to say how very sorry I am for messing up so badly. I know it was a really stupid mistake and very unprofessional of me. I can understand if you don't want me around the company anymore but I was hoping that maybe you would allow me to come in to the office and help out in some way? I'm not sure what I could do but I'm willing to learn and I'm sure I could be of some help."

Chris just looked at me and then responded gracefully. "Dom, don't be silly. We all make mistakes sometimes. That's how we learn. I don't have much I can give you now but can you stand on your feet?"

"Sure, err, at least I think so," I said, wondering where this was heading.

"Great, because I really need someone to paint the offices. Maybe you can start with that and we'll see how it goes. I can give you a couple of hundred bucks every week. Will that work for you?"

"Definitely," I responded enthusiastically. This was not what I was expecting but in another way, it was more than I had expected. At least I could pay rent and have enough for transport and food for the next few months until my leg healed.

That evening when I went home I could not believe my good fortune. I wasn't fired from the company for my mistake. I was being given a second chance. I could stay connected to this great opportunity. This was the first time I had been shown some compassion in a business environment. This act of generosity helped forge an extremely powerful business and personal relationship between us.

Business Lesson 22

All business can be personal. If you treat people in your business like you would treat your friends or family members and help them out in time of need then you might be surprised at the hard work and loyalty you receive in return.

Learning the insides of the Business

Even though I was now the office painter, I still went to the office every morning at 7:00 a.m. dressed in my suit. I wanted to be in all the meetings and keep in touch with what was going on. I really enjoyed the great atmosphere and my new friendships; I didn't want to miss out on all the action. Once everyone left for the field around 9:00 a.m. I would swiftly change into my work clothes.

I would motivate the rest of the team by explaining how eager I was to get back out there. They could go out and make money everyday and build their teams. I was stuck on crutches in the office and would have loved to be in their position.

My personal team had dwindled down to only three members and I could see that they were dropping off fast. They hadn't yet made enough sales to be promoted to leader and I could see that without someone looking after them their numbers would probably decline pretty quickly. There wasn't much I could do except to ask Steve to try to help them out. He did but he was busy focusing on his stronger team members who were showing more ambition and drive to grow.

It only took me a week to finish all the painting in the office, light blue walls and dark blue trim. It looked like a fish bowl; correct that, a professional fish bowl. My expertise was in striping roads and parking lots, not in painting offices. Chris could see I was moving around without much difficulty on my crutches. I was helping out the administration team with inventory control. They were teaching me how to do the Daily Master, which balanced the sales with the cash and split up the various sales tax percentages on each item.

I was thinking about how I could design some helpful tools for the sales team. This was before Excel spreadsheets had come along so I used a pen (we had plenty of them) a ruler and a piece of blank paper.

I created a spreadsheet for the sales team that was easy to keep folded in their pocket and they could use the whole week. This way we could keep count of how many people they were pitching and when their sales were made. During my three weeks in the field, I had pitched close to 5000 people and had started to notice some patterns about the timing of my sales.

I noticed that you could be pitching for hours without a sale. Then boom, finally someone would buy from you and like magic within the next two or three pitches there would be more sales. So the sales were clustered in a way. I wondered if this was due to the randomness of finding an interested customer or more to do with the fact that after a sale was made the salesperson's confidence, attitude and belief in their product shot up so much that it carried this combined enthusiasm over to the next customer.

I also noticed that there were certain types of trends over the course of a day. For instance, some days I had sales very early on then maybe a slump in the afternoon, then more sales at the end of the day. On other days, I didn't find buyers until late in the afternoon and would never have found them had I given up. These were the days when following the system and believing in the Law of Averages was so important.

Unfortunately, most new salespeople stopped working on these days or left their territories to try their luck somewhere else. Skipping their area was a terrible habit because it went against our 7 Steps to Success system, which ultimately would break down our company's system of working.

If I could just show them factually, statistically how many different types of days there were and how the more experienced salespeople had the same trends but stuck at their territory and ended up making sales by the end of the day; then I knew they would be more apt to stay motivated throughout the day, stick to the 5 Step and 7 Step systems and ultimately make more sales.

I wanted to try to help the new people get focused on becoming a trainer/leader as soon as possible. I started brainstorming with some of the top trainers and team builders and then checked with Chris regarding the main areas on which they needed to focus.

It was important for new trainees to communicate with the right people who could help them with advice on improving their skills. They needed to learn about personal and professional responsibility with regards to timekeeping and money management. They needed to be responsible for their daily inventory and show care for their merchandise. Their personal and professional image including how well they presented themselves to their customers and represented our company. The other big focus was how well they maintained their attitude towards customers and colleagues. Were they positive around the office and in the field?

Most importantly, they needed to learn our system, the 5-Steps to a Sale (The Pitch Method) and The 7- Steps to Success (Good Work Habits). If they followed our tried and proven system then they would make adequate sales and be profitable. After a brainstorming session we were able to come up with an acronym so it was easy to remember and keep top of mind. New trainees needed to grasp the basics and show consistency in these five areas and ultimately they could be promoted to a Trainee Management position in as little as one week, just like I had done.

G.R.A.S.P.

G = Get with people.

R = Responsibility for yourself and your merchandise.

A =Attitude – you must have a great attitude to be successful in a sales and people business.

S = System - You've got to know and be able to work your system.

P = Profitability – if you can do these things then your profitability will come and you will be able to become a trainer and build your own team.

I designed a chart with all these focus points listed across the top of the page and split up with little boxes you could tick off for each day of the week. If you followed it consistently and had a positive $\sqrt{}$ = complete (great job) instead of an x= incomplete (needs work) in the box regularly each day for a whole week then you would inevitably get promoted by the end of the week.

These worksheets put the newly recruited and trained sales agents in control of their advancement. It helped them focus their mental energy on the task at hand. We all needed everyone we trained to become successful or we wouldn't be able to hit our goals to become managers of our own offices and directors of our own businesses.

Interviews anyone? Thrown in the deep end.

The office was getting busier and busier. Jeff 's team was growing quickly at nearly twenty people strong. The "Brisbane Bound!" chants filled our morning motivational meetings. Their team's weekly sales were quickly reaching the ten thousand dollar mark needed to hit Jeff's goal to be the first Australian owner – well, first Canadian/Australian owner.

Chris was investing in as many classified ads as the business could afford. He was under big pressure to come up with enough suitable candidates to supply his ever-growing team of trainee managers. Their appetites were becoming voracious. They needed to get as many new recruits as they could to build there "own teams" and get their "own offices." If Jeff was taking Brisbane then it was just a matter of time before Melbourne, Perth and Adelaide were gone. The race was on to grab the remaining major metropolises.

One morning Chris called me into the office and asked if I thought I could conduct an interview? I told him I wasn't sure since I had been only a participant on a few occasions. He said, "Well, do you want to try?"

"Of course I do"

Okay," he replied. "Let's do a quick mock interview and I'll show you how it's done and what questions to ask." He then proceeded to interview me and showed me how to walk someone through the application form.

The key to interviewing people for our business was to motivate them to come in the next day so they could be shown how we work. Because we worked on commission only (we called it a price mark-up system), we wanted to avoid the question "how do I get paid?" if at all possible in the first interview. We knew that if they spent a full day with one of our top sales agents (Trainee Manager's) they would easily see how much of a mark-up could be earned and then realize how they could make much more on our system than a salary or hourly payment.

The idea was to see if they had the personality and drive required so we could get them in and show how we worked. We could rely on the strength of the trainer to show them a great day and motivate them towards trying out the business.

This is easier said than done and to my surprise, we were not the only company to run this type of structure. I quickly found out that some people knew more about how we worked than I did.

After a five-minute role-play, and much to my surprise, Chris said, "Okay, you're ready. You can interview the first few people this morning at 11:00 and then I'll pitch in and help out if you need a hand later in the afternoon."

This was his intention but was not how the day turned out. By the time I helped with inventory count and straightened up the meeting room, I got a call from reception that I already had a few people waiting for interviews. When I entered the reception area a few more were arriving. I looked in Chris's office and noticed that he was in a meeting so I took the initiative and called in my first interview.

He was a young guy in his mid thirties and, like most people, had already done a few jobs but had no sales experience. When I asked him what attracted him to the position he just answered, "When I looked at your ad, it says that you need forty people so that's why I responded. Do you have any jobs in the warehouse?"

This is when I realized that I should have read the ad before I started doing interviews. "Ah, no. Actually we're not. I just started helping out with interviews on the spur of the moment and as you can see I'm on crutches so we're actually looking for people to do the job I was doing up until my accident."

I explained to him that at the moment we were looking for people to learn the sales first and then move up in the company once they learned the basics. I explained to him how I'd been promoted to a trainee manager within my first week and had already started building my own team.

He was completely uninterested and said that he wasn't ambitious and was actually very upset about or advertisement because he thought it was misleading. I told him that I would talk to the owner of the business this afternoon and see if there were any opportunities in the warehouse and would look into changing the ad.

When we finished the interview and I walked him to the door. I peered into the lobby. There were another ten people waiting. My stomach started knotting up and I could only think, *I had better hustle up! Where's Chris? Do I have to do all of these by myself? And what's the story with our ad?*

The answers I discovered were – yes, I'd better hustle up; Chris is busy; yes, you have to do all of these interviews by yourself and the ad says you have forty jobs including sales, warehousing duties, administration, assistant managers and managers.

For the next five hours I interviewed over thirty people. By the end of the day I was more worn out than when I was out selling in the field. At least when I was out selling in the field I could take a break if I wanted to. With people waiting impatiently all day I knew I had to first win them over and calm them down before I delicately handled the misleading ad issue. I quickly learned to explain how we were accepting applications for warehousing duties, administration, assistant management and management but right now we were looking for people that could learn the sales side first and then move through the other aspects of the business as our company grew. I found that if I stressed less on the sales and more on the growth aspects they became a bit more enthusiastic about working with us.

I interviewed people of all ages, skill levels, experience and expectations. Each person was a personal challenge to try to persuade him or her to do entry-level sales. Once I finally convinced them that it was worth their time to give it a shot they would immediately ask, "How do I get paid? Is it commission only?"

After stumbling through this deadly question in my first few interviews, I remembered to utilize some of my sales experience. I found that if I started to move quickly to my next positive but challenging question like, - "Have you ever managed people before? And if so, please tell me about your experiences. If not then do you think you could learn how if you were trained?" - Then they would often forget to ask the question concerning their compensation.

And before they had the chance, I would interrupt by saying, "As I said earlier, this is just a preliminary interview and as you can see there are a lot of people

190

waiting in the reception. Based on what we've talked about so far I would like to invite you back on an observation day tomorrow. This is where you'll get a chance to see what we're all about, ask a lot more questions and, of course, it gives us an opportunity to evaluate you and see if you're the right fit for our company. How does that sound?"

Ninety-five percent of the time interviewees would agree to this and I could then move on to set the appointment time and the expectations of the observation day. They left feeling good and I put everything off until the next day. This tactic worked great as long as it was coupled with a confirmation call in the evening from our administrative staff.

The call went something like this: "Thanks for coming in today. As you already know, the manager interviewed quite a few people this afternoon and you were short-listed for the observation day tomorrow. I just wanted to confirm your appointment and make sure you know to come in ten minutes early so we can prep you for the day."

This confirmation call was instrumental to the whole process. Eight times out of ten, it solidified the appointment. There was always a fall off of potential applicants once they had a chance to get home, digest the information covered in the interview and talked with friends or family. Some inevitable questions always seemed to pop up. - "What does the company do? What's the job on offer? How much does it pay?"

Friend and family responses usually went something like this, "Sales? You can't do sales!" Or, "Sounds pretty shady to me. You didn't give them your bank details did you?" Or even this one: "My brother/uncle/best friend/cousin did something like that and didn't make any money. It's probably one of those pyramid scams."

We tried to do everything within our means to mitigate the drop off rate. When new recruits failed to show up on time the next day we would start calling them again to see if we could get them in later or for the next day. Considering this I still I had about an eighty-five percent retention rate on my first day interviewing. When I asked Chris why we didn't put ads in the newspaper which stated the exact job description, he told me that he had tried it and got so few responses that it wouldn't work at the moment with our current recruitment needs. We needed people fast.

"Think about your experience, Dom. If the ad had read, "Commission-only sales job with a huge opportunity to own your own company", would you have believe it? Would you have answered it?"

Before I could answer, he explained that the best way to recruit was to interview and talk to as many people as possible, to use our people skills to develop a rapport then get them out working and show them the possibilities. If they liked it and thought they could do it, half the battle was won. If not, at least the trainee managers got more experience and had a chance to improve their teambuilding skills.

"Plus," he added, "most people have a pre-conceived mostly negative view about this type of work and could never imagine themselves doing it much less having fun while doing so. Our job is to get them in and introduced to the right trainer so they can show them a great day of having fun and making money. If they're the right fit for us then we'll both know. Normally we only ever attract the more ambitious type of person looking to experience something new."

I completely understood his recruiting method and liked his way of looking at it because it really worked well to attract me only a month prior.

"I always look for three things in people," Chris said. "One, do they have a good attitude? Two, are they willing to learn? And three, can they work without supervision? If they say yes to all three of these then I ask them back for an observation day."

"Got it!" I said. I was ready to roll.

After I got over the realization that I would have been asked back instantly anyway and that I had not been duped but simply introduced to something different in a kind of traditional way, I was able to get more focused on becoming a better interviewer. The process made a lot more sense to me when he explained it that way. I just had to get geared up to look at the interview process like I did in the field. I should present the job in the best way possible and see if I could quickly build trust and interest.

As it turned out, Chris had already replaced himself. He left me to do all the interviews while he worked on building other aspects of his business. He was happy to be freed up from this necessary daily duty while I was happy to learn, grow and contribute in any way I could.

This went on for several weeks. I noticed that as I became more confident and knowledgeable about the business and how to present it, my retention was getting worse. Perhaps I was coming across too smooth and too confident. I wasn't really relating to people and wasn't giving them a chance to express themselves. I needed to make them feel more like they had earned the right to come back for an observation day, just like I felt during my interview. People never told me this directly. They just went along with everything and didn't show up for the observation.

Business Lesson 22

People have a sixth sense. They can tell whether or not you're paying attention to them, love the sound of your own voice or are just going through the motions.

I had to re-train myself using the adage, "People don't care how much I know until they know how much I care." I changed my approach and told more of my story and encouraged them to give me more details about theirs. I talked about my first three weeks in the business before my accident and how I wished with all my might that I could be out there building my own team. I stressed how great the company was to actually give me a chance to stay and learn the other aspects of the management-training program. People started responding and it was getting real again. They started showing up for their second appointment and the trainers were noticing how ready they were to learn the business and get started.

Everyday, I was learning about business and growing

in terms of my management and people skills. I had the chance to experiment with different interview techniques and approaches then reflect on my results. Life was good and challenging which made me feel extremely happy and honored to have this great opportunity.

"Only two things make money, people and money."
Colin Gerrard

CHAPTER 19 LEARNING POINTS:

LIFE and BUSINESS WISDOM

Always ask clearly for what you want and you'll be surprised how often you get it.

Do more than what you get paid for and eventually you'll get paid for more than what you do.

Success is an ongoing journey. Keep learning and growing as you go along and know that you'll never arrive at a permanent destination but you will certainly visit many wonderful spots along the way.

Sometimes you have to use persuasive strategies to entice people to join your business or see your perspective. It's "OK" to use all your personal power if you have their best interests at heart and keep to your word.

When it's time to part company do so with grace. Wish them all the best in the future and mean it.

CHAPTER 20

Crazy Fast Expansion and A Buzzing Atmosphere

The office atmosphere was explosive. Steve and Jeff were building their teams like crazy while other trainers were starting to pick up the basics and grow their teams as well. Some of the newest additions like Stewart, a traveller from the UK, started to figure out the sales and team-building really quickly. Other fast learners were Troy, Angelo, Tony, Marcus, Cheryl, Phil and Nick.

Everyone had his or her own story and reasons for getting excited about the opportunity to build their own team and open their own offices. Chris was amping up the trainers meetings and running marathon sessions on Monday nights to make sure everyone was learning and getting their minds conditioned for growth. As more people joined and came up with bigger goals, so did Chris. He matched his goals to theirs. He started thinking bigger and sharing a larger vision. He didn't just talk about opening cities but we now spoke about expanding to new countries.

I would open in the USA; Harvey would open in London, and Phil would start in Adelaide and then expand to his hometown of Hobart. The travellers from Europe wanted to open their offices in Australia and make their fortunes first before returning back to their own country to either retire or continue the expansion.

Some of the trainers started to openly compete to see who would be the first to open in a new city. Tony and Nick were racing for Perth. Stewart and Taras were competing to open another office in Sydney while Cheryl was quietly planning on beating them both. Marcus and Patrick were competing to open the first office in Auckland, New Zealand.

Meanwhile, it was Jeff who was solidifying his team and going for his sales target to reach his first week's production. I was interviewing like crazy to help him find some suitable candidates to join his ever-expanding team. It was a very exciting time. We were working like crazy but enjoying ourselves immensely. Our motto was, "Have fun and make money." It was as simple as that. And so many of our potential candidates were picking up on this great office atmosphere and joining in just to see if what we were talking about would actually come true.

Business Lesson 23

"Seeing is believing" won't work when your building something new that doesn't exist. Rather "Believing is seeing". You must have blind faith - Believe first what you want to create. Work like crazy for it and then you'll see it. Never wait on the sidelines or someone else will create it and by then it'll be too late.

So many people have to see it to believe it. Our core leadership team was working this concept in reverse. We had no choice but to actually believe it in order to see it. We somehow understood that we were moving in unchartered territory and that it was up to us to keep our dreams alive. Our positive attitude and unyielding belief in our own success would attract and hold people on our teams, which in turn would enable us to get our offices.

Chris was constantly encouraging everyone to think bigger, pitch bigger, talk bigger, dream bigger and this was giving everyone extra fuel to allay any doubts we might have had whether this was even possible.

There was no room for naysayers in our office. People were having fun and making money everyday. Of course there were a few who didn't but we knew it was because they weren't working the system. So we would all literally gang up on them in a positive way in the evening and give them a small "impact" (sales coaching session) and let them know they would get a re-train the next day with one of the top trainers. We ensured them that they would be back on track by the end of the retrain day.

We would get them out with one of our top people and show them how to make a hundred and fifty dollars so they could learn the skill, or the way, or the attitude they needed to be able to do it for themselves after the re-train. This kept people coming back for more and encouraged them to stick at the sales until they got it.

Anyone who was consistently negative would be removed from the office.

We never gave up on anyone as long as they:

1) Had a positive attitude.

2) Kept listening, learning and applying our training and advice.

3) Kept putting in effort to improve and showed commitment by showing up everyday.

Jeff's promotion and my continued education

Jeff's crew and sales kept cranking up. He easily hit his two-week production (Team Sales Target of $10,000 turnover two weeks in a row) and got promoted to assistant manager. This meant that he would earn four percent of the entire office's turnover. This money would go into his office savings account until he had enough saved to incorporate his business and open his own office in Brisbane.

Jeff would now learn all the things he needed to know to run his own office – what went on in the inside of the business to support the growth in the field. He would learn the administration, which covered warehouse control, inventory tracking, pricing, sales taxes, and filling out ledgers for bookkeeping. He would also learn the recruiting side of the business, including how to write advertisements and conduct interviews, how to do call backs and how to handle the incoming calls. He would learn how to build relationships with key people in our business community including professional advisers, bankers, accountants and lawyers. It was important to build solid relationships, not just with your team but with their families, too. Often family members would end up working as support staff in our ever-growing business.

When Jeff came in from the field to learn his new duties this freed me up to do, what? *Oh no,* I thought, *what can I do now?*

Chris and I brainstormed some possibilities. One of the things we hadn't considered yet was how to shift more of our stock faster. We were only selling through our field force but we were always pitching as if we could supply businesses on a larger scale. We were bringing in larger and larger quantities of certain products that were just sitting in our warehouse. Some of the items weren't suitable for carrying out all day in the field.

I understood from Chris that the company was shipping items from some of their offices in the USA and Canada that hadn't sold too well or were somewhat outdated. We were acting as a kind of dumping ground for these items. Pitching is pitching, we thought. "So why don't I try to call up some of the importers, wholesalers and larger retail chains? I could make appointments and bring samples to show them," I suggested. Obviously, I couldn't drive as I was still on crutches but Chris said I could just hop in a cab.

We had nothing to lose if it worked. *Yet another comfort zone to smash through,* I thought. *How do I make this happen?*

Like I mentioned before, Chris was one of those people who naturally thinks that if someone else could do something, then so could he. Neither one of us had ever sold merchandise to importers or big retailers but it was worth a shot. Doing this would keep me actively helping the company grow while I was in my current condition.

Chris once again gave me a crash course on what I should say to get an appointment. His advice was to use the same five-step approach we used on the field and just adapt it a bit over the phone to make an appointment. So I grabbed the phone book and went to work.

My calls went something like this: "Hi, this is Dominic Kotarski calling from Global Imports. I would like to speak to the buyer please."

"May I ask what this is concerning?"

"Uh, yeah, I'm calling from Global Imp…"

"Oh, no thanks, we've got our own suppliers and do not take appointments over the phone." Click.

Okay, Dom, you're a bit rusty. This isn't going to be easy. Remember what you've learned. Create curiosity, build impulse and make sure the gatekeeper feels like she or he better connect you to their boss or buyer and if they don't, they will be either making a big mistake or feel like their missing out on a great opportunity. Don't forget to be yourself and connect with them on a personal level. Have fun. The pressure is not on you it's on them. Use the structure you learned. You can do this. Also, it doesn't matter if you mess up as you can always try again. Remember, it's the law of averages. All my training and all my advice I'd been given and had been giving to the new people in the office were starting to kick in. *Okay, try again and believe you can do it this time!* I told myself as I picked up the telephone.

"Hi, this is Dom Kotarski from Global Imports, one of Australia's newest and fastest growing importers. We're bringing in excellent items at great prices. Can I make an appointment to come and show you what we've got?" I felt like I was talking a million miles an hour.

"Excuse me, who is this and what did you say?" This was my cue to slow down, speak clearly and just connect. *Dom, relax; be confident and pull yourself together,* I reminded myself.

"I'm sorry. My name is Dom Kotarski and I'm calling from our offices here in Alexandria. I would like to speak to your buyer if I could?" Pause.

"May I ask what this is concerning?"

"Yes, we're an importer that's expanding very quickly in Australia. We've got a multi-million dollar business in the USA and Canada and are bringing in large quantities of merchandise. Our buying power is very strong and I would like to make an appointment to come and see your buyer to show some of our samples."

"Uh, wait just a moment." Long pause.

I was feeling very uncomfortable doing this over the phone. I could tell the administrator was busy and her manager probably was too. I had to connect in some way and build curiosity enough for them to schedule an appointment.

"I just talked to our buyer and he said you could call back in half an hour."

"Great and who am I speaking to?

"Oh, this is Anna."

"Hi Anna. I'm sorry for being so abrupt when I rang. I don't normally make calls from the office and your voice sounded like you were really busy so I wanted to make sure I didn't hold you up too long."

"Oh, it's crazy around here. Sometimes I am too abrupt."

"Well, Anna, I won't keep you. I'll give you a call back in around thirty minutes anyway."

Now that's better, I thought. *Speak slowly, build rapport, keep it brief but make it interesting.*

CHAPTER 20 LEARNING POINTS:

LIFE and BUSINESS WISDOM

From the first explorers to today's entrepreneurs having an unyielding and consistent belief in your vision is paramount to attracting a team and maintaining positive growth.

Success awaits those that consistently put themselves in situations where they might fail or look foolish.

There's always a way to solve a problem and create an opportunity.

Most people are problem avoiders. They try to ignore them or run away. Those that see problems as future opportunities end up running the world.

CHAPTER 21

Buyers don't behave like ordinary people

It's one thing to sell products to unsuspecting customers. When you're pitted up against seasoned professional buyers you need to be prepared to change your tactics and up your game.

There are certain aspects of human behavior we all have in common. These "human impulse" characteristics lie in the emotional/feeling realm. We trained our sales people to try to tap into their prospects emotions as much as possible when presenting their products and services. We ran impact meetings (Sales Training Sessions) at least once a week on this topic. We created an acronym to easily remember these impulse factors and if all five were incorporated in your pitch then undoubtedly both you and your customer would receive G.I.F.T.S. (you would get your sale and they would get your products – (Nice Result)

G = Greed

I = Indifference

F = Fear of loss

T = The sense of urgency

S = Sheep factor

A perfect pitch that built massive impulse in the customer incorporated these five human impulses.

Greed – People love a good deal and hate to miss

out on a bargain. Make sure your pitch appeals to this natural human emotion.

Indifference – This is something that you can portray as the salesperson. Make it appear that you're successful and your product is selling with or without your current prospect's decision to buy. You care that your prospect gets to have a great product at a great price but you know your going to sell out with or without their business.

Fear of loss – There are limited quantities of your products and because it's such a good deal it will run out soon so the customer should ACT NOW!

The Sense of Urgency – A continuation of the fear of loss. 'If you ACT NOW then you won't have to feel the pain of regret, knowing that you could have had this wonderful deal and great opportunity but didn't act so you missed out. Best thing is to buy now to avoid this awful feeling of regret.'

Sheep Factor – You're not alone; you're not the only one taking advantage of this great deal. This is social proofing. Sheep follow sheep even off cliffs. It's a safe feeling. It also says, you're smart; you're not a sucker. Everyone's doing it so you should to. The "everyone" who is doing it is smart and clever for doing so. By joining them, you're not alone and you're an intelligent buyer.

I would eventually get all of these elements into my calls if I had to in order to get the appointments. I got better and better the more calls I made. I would call back the same numbers the next day at different times if my first attempts weren't successful. Because I was in the office early and always left late, I could sometimes by-pass the receptionist or gatekeeper and get straight to the owner of the company.

Business Lesson 24

If you're willing to be the first in and the last to leave, and you use this extra time to experiment with unconventional business practices - go beyond acceptable social norms - you will beat 90% of your competitors. This is the true meaning of "going the extra- mile.

Now that I had my appointment book full, I had to work out how to sell our products in bulk. On my first day of appointments, I knew that it was up to me to make it happen. Chris had given me all the tools I needed. He let me take the ledger with me that showed our actual landed prices. This was the actual price of the product after we included all the costs of import duties, shipping and freight to get the product into our warehouse. Basically it was the bottom line price. Any price above our landed cost would be profit for the company. All I had to do was make sure I negotiated above that mark.

I wanted to bring as many product samples as I could. Some of them were hot sellers for us in the field and I knew that it wouldn't be beneficial to sell them below the cost that our merchandisers were getting them for. We could sell them successfully anyway and get our margins. It was good to bring these products along to the meeting because I could show them what "hot" sellers for us were at the moment. As well, I could gauge what their buying power was versus ours, if they had ever imported a similar item. Buying power was normally determined by quantities bought. If you were a big player then you probably bought items in the hundreds of thousands, or even millions, depending upon your market. The more you bought, the better the price you could get from the manufacturer.

My first day of appointments was a disaster. It was so awkward for me to get in and out of cabs on crutches while trying to carry a huge box of samples without spilling them everywhere. I also realized that I was way out of my comfort and knowledge zones. The appointments went like this:

I would go in and introduce myself. The buyers were much older than me and didn't seem to be impressed with my youthfulness. They didn't care about my story, my company or me. They were unimpressed with almost everything. They had unblinking eyes and showed absolutely no emotion on their faces.

They would ask to see what I had and as I brought out the product they would either pick it up and look at it or just stare at it for a brief moment and say, "How much?"

I wasn't at all prepared for this. I would immediately flip through my journal and glance line by line until I found the item. I would then look across the page and add about twenty or thirty percent to the price. I knew they were importers themselves so I didn't want to pitch too high, otherwise they would think I was an idiot.

When I would tell them the price they just wouldn't

say a word. They wouldn't blink; they wouldn't make any expression whatsoever. They would just say something like, "What else you got?"

That was it. This would carry on until I had shown them every single product in my box. They then would say, "Is that it?"

When I answered, "Yes, at the moment," they would say, "Okay. Well, your prices are way too high and we're not interested in anything you have. Let us know if you get anything new and, oh yeah, thanks for coming."

I was in and out in the amount of time it took to go through this process. I was back at the office after three appointments with nothing to show for my effort except over a hundred dollars in cab fares.

When I got back and told Chris how the appointments had gone, he had a few suggestions but nothing really tangible.

"Did you try to get the product in their hands?"

"Did you tell them that these were our hot items?"

"Did you ask them, how many they were interested in before you told them the price?"

"Did you tell them how big a buyer we were in Hong Kong?"

"Yes," I answered to all the questions. "I had tried all of that but there was just no reaction. I didn't have any clue about where we stood with them? If they did say anything after I showed an item and revealed the price they just said, "Too high!" That was it. As far as we go in this market our prices are way too high.

We were both dumbfounded. "How do you know that our buying power was all that good?" I asked.

"Well, I'm pretty sure it is," Chris responded, "but I'm not too sure how to handle this situation. Let's see if we can get Barry on the phone."

I knew the name, Barry, because Chris had mentioned him in quite a few of his meetings. Barry was the master. He was the driving force behind the expansion in Canada and the USA. Barry had given Chris the opportunity to go to Australia and expand the company. He was Chris's mentor in the company. He was the one giving the guidance and advice to make our expansion happen in Australia.

I realized then that what Steve was to me Barry was to Chris. We all had mentors at different levels in the business. Steve was my mentor to learn sales and team building. Chris had taken over to teach me the skills to run the office from the inside. Barry was teaching Chris how to run his own country. I was getting a chance to get advice from another extremely successful businessman. Barry was already a multi-millionaire and one of the founders of the company based out of Canada that was providing us with this great opportunity.

I wondered what he could actually teach me in this situation that would be helpful. It certainly didn't seem to me that there was anything I could have done any differently that would have helped me to get a better outcome. Clearly, our buying power wasn't what we thought it was and we should stick to just selling in small quantities with our tried and proven method. I was about to find out that this was not the case at all. Things are not always as they seem.

210

The Game of Business is about execution

There is a reason that not all intelligent people are rich. University professors know the subject of business better than most entrepreneurs. They can teach all day about the best practices and draw insightful conclusions out of research. What they often can't do is teach students how to execute, how to alter their normal behavior in business situations in order to come out on top in a business negotiation. This is difficult for the average person to do much less teach.

That is why there are thousands of successful business people who feel compelled to write books about what they don't teach you at Harvard Business School, and other prestigious colleges and universities. Many graduates of even these top business institutions feel somewhat cheated after they spend all their time and money only to flounder their first few years in the business world because they feel and act like complete novices. I certainly felt like I had missed something at business school and it wasn't from skipping my classes.

When we called Barry from our office speakerphone it was 10:00 p.m. his time and he was ready to talk. He seemed to have no personal and business boundaries.

"Hi Barry. This is Chris. I've got Dom with me and we wanted to ask your advice on something."

"Sure," Barry said, "what's happening, or rather, not happening?"

We explained the situation and Barry just listened until we finished giving him all the reasons why I was having difficulty getting these buyers to respond.

Halfway through our explanation, he had heard enough.

"Dom, here's what you're going to do in the next meeting. You have to do exactly what I say and we'll be able to find out if our prices are competitive or not and possibly be able to start getting some business."

"Okay, Mr. Thalmann," I said.

"Call me Barry. Here's what you do. Go into the meeting just as you've been doing. If the buyer doesn't react or says, the price is too high or whatever, you take out your next item and quote him a price that's fifty percent below our landed price."

"What if he takes me up on it?" I asked, a bit confused.

"He won't. Remember, this is a game and you have to get them engaged. They're just feeling you out, fishing for our prices, shopping but have no intention on buying anything."

"Okay, sure. I've got it. Then what?"

"You get up from your chair, pack up all your products and leave," Barry said.

I laughed. Barry got really intense on the phone. I could sense him getting upset. "Listen guys," he said, "I'm not joking. If you want to do business, you've got to do it this way. Remember, you called me and the way you're going about this isn't working. You're wasting your time, their time and now my time."

"I'm sorry, Barry," I said, soberly. "I wasn't laughing at you. I just don't see how this will work. I'll be walking out within the first few minutes of the appointment. How rude would that be? I'm the one that asked them for the appointment and now I'm rudely getting up and walking out?"

"Exactly, and that's why what I'm about to tell you is so powerful," Barry continued.

"When you stand up to leave, look him or her straight in the eye and say, 'I'm here to do business with you and you're here to rob me.' Can you do that?"

"Uh, yeah, I suppose so," I fumbled.

"You can't suppose so and you can't do it halfway. You must have conviction in your voice and your body language when you say it. Trust me when I say if you do this right you will do business. If not, they were a waste of time anyway."

I had just had my first grown-up business lesson after all my positive, upbeat enthusiastic business experiences up to this moment. I was scared and I wasn't sure if I could do what Barry had proposed but I had appointments booked for the following day. I needed to get my head around how I was going to do these meetings.

There was no way I could come back to Chris with the same lame excuses. I knew I must get some sleep and come in with a new conviction. I must follow the advice of the founder of the company. Who was I to question something from someone who obviously had much more experience dealing with these kinds of situations than I?

Chris got educated, too. He didn't know at the time how to advise me and Barry had just given us both a lesson in business. I wasn't comfortable with what I had to do but I had learned so many things in the past three months about creating transactions with people, I thought I might as well keep the learning curve growing.

CHAPTER 21 LEARNING POINTS:

LIFE and BUSINESS WISDOM

Every profession has deeper levels of sophistication, if you aspire to reach the top of your profession you have to be willing to make the personal sacrifices in order to get access to those levels, as well as bucket loads of perseverance, intensity, luck, passion and intelligence.

Business lessons are repeated until learned; seek out mentors to shorten your lesson and learning curve.

You are an actor on the business stage - the better you learn your role and those of your colleagues, adversaries, business associates, customers and prospects the more successful you'll be at creating the outcome you prefer; learn to execute with authority and impact.

CHAPTER 22

Putting it all together

I got a good night's sleep that night and woke feeling refreshed. Chris was on fire in the morning meeting and talked about the fact that we're learning and growing everyday. He mentioned the fact that we should strive to be more humble, as there was a lot created before we were born. He talked about how he was still learning everyday from people who were higher up in the business than he and how he kept asking questions to better his business and grow it to the next level. He shared stories about other movers and shakers in the business who had grown to become financially independent in a fairly short period of time.

My own thoughts were drifting back to some of the lessons I had learned and read about in university. I was inspired by one of my economics professors who talked about the difference between academia and the real world.

It was about bravery and taking risks. This was something that entrepreneurs had to learn to balance well. He spoke about how great entrepreneurs were scared too but something inside them drove them to temporarily suspend their fears long enough to execute their plans.

I was determined to try out this new tactic that Barry

had advocated. I was scared. I feared going against my upbringing. All those proper manners that had been drilled into me since before I could talk. Still, I was going to deliver this line if the opportunity arose. I wanted to be successful and I shouldn't question advice I hadn't tried out for myself. I wanted to own my own success, on my own terms and this meant operating out of my comfort zone.

"When the student is ready the teacher will be there." *Buddhist proverb*

Life often surprises us and delivers us the opportunities we need to grow, exactly when we need them.

I made it to my appointment a bit early and was greeted by a young man in reception.

"Oh yes, the owner is expecting you," he said. "He's just finishing with a client and will be with you shortly. Please come through to our showroom and he'll be right with you."

As I walked through, I could see a small round table with a couple of chairs next to it. I made my way to the table as professionally as possible considering my crutches and my awkward sample box. Luckily, he noticed and gave me a hand. Just as I started to sit down the owner walked in.

"Good day, mate. How did you find out about us?"

I could see that he was in his late forties or early fifties and very confident and business savvy. He had an impressive-looking business and was obviously well established. I felt intimidated but was used to that feeling by now and went straight into banter mode to try to hide my insecurity.

"Um, through the yellow pages. You've got quite a big ad running," I responded.

"Yeah, righto. Gotta pay to play! So, what brings you here?"

"Well, we're importers too, and we've just recently landed quite a few new items that we aren't moving through our traditional channels yet. I thought I could show you what we've got and see if there's anything we could do together." This just seemed to roll off my tongue. I was happy not to stumble too much. My nerves were steady and I knew what I was about to do or prepared to do if the opportunity arose. We were just sitting down as this conversation was unfolding.

"So, let's see what you've got!" he demanded.

I liked this guy. He was a bit more energetic and personable than the previous day's bunch. I was getting more relaxed and was fairly certain this conversation would go smoothly and I wouldn't have to "deliver the line".

Imagine my surprise, when I pulled out my first product and his demeanor instantly changed. His animation and smile disappeared as he switched his personality into buyer mode. I was starting to wonder if all these buyers went to some sort of buyer's school where they teach how to make sales people feel uncomfortable, unwanted, and out of place.

I pulled out my first product. I was a bit more prepared this time and knew the landed price plus thirty percent without having to look it up in my ledger.

Just like my experiences from the day before he picked it up for about a second, placed it back down on the table, looked at me with expressionless eyes and asked "How much?"

I looked down at my ledger, ran my finger down the column and without having to actually find the item in the ledger quoted him a price.

Right on cue, he frowned and said, "Too high! What else you got?"

I pulled out my next item from the box and placed it on the table in front of him. My nerves were at their peak and my heart was beating so hard I'm sure he could hear it. I prayed he doesn't just look at it and ask the price.

"How much?"

I have reached the point of no return. I glanced down at the ledger, scroll my finger down the ledger, holding it just at enough of an angle that he can't snoop and see our landed price.

"$3.50." My voice quavered. *Get it together, Dom,* I tell myself silently. *It's just a game.* Get ready to grab your crutches and stand up from the table. My heart was beating like crazy.

"Too high. You got anything else?" he responded.

Everything appeared to go in slow motion then I reached for my crutches, pushed myself up from the table and glanced toward him as I'm gaining upward momentum.

"I'm here to do business and it appears that you're here to rob me!" I said in a calm voice.

I can't believe I said this; I can't believe I'm doing this, I thought. It felt so bad, so wrong, so against my trained and ingrained social manners.

Whew! He reached out with both hands as if he's trying to grab me. *Don't flinch Dom,* I thought.

"I'm just looking to get a feel for your prices and buying power. I'm not trying to rob you." His manner transformed slightly. He acted as if he'd hurt my feelings or something.

My face must have been bright red from embarrassment but I think he interpreted it as anger. I held my look and spoke fiercely, "I quoted you fifty percent below my landed cost. We are some of the biggest buyers of this item in Hong Kong. There's no way this price is too high. We've got over fifty offices in North America selling our products. If this price is too high then there's no way we could ever do business." I was on fire.

He immediately changed his demeanor and calmly said, "Mate, please grab a seat and let's look at what else you have. My apologies for appearing rude but you know I get so many salesman in here everyday trying to flog stuff and I've got to find out if they can do real business or not."

After this fired-up exchange, our real rapport began. I walked out of his office an hour later with an order to deliver 6,500 pieces and a cheque for over $21,000! I had learned so many valuable lessons in the last few months but this was one of the most valuable.

Sometimes in business you've got to go against the norms of social behavior in order to build a better working rapport. You've got to be prepared to walk away from the deal in order to get that deal. These were the same skills I had developed previously while going business to business. It was a combination of showing indifference on my behalf and creating fear of loss on the buyers. I learned that the same principles of a sale were present regardless of the size of the transaction and the parties involved.

People are people. Everyone's thoughts and emotions are designed to move toward pleasure – toward the things that we need, want and desire – and to move away from pain – the consequences we don't want or the things we want to avoid.

I went back to the office that afternoon on a massive high. I knew I had changed in some ways. I had grown up. Three months previously, I had left America looking for a chance or an opportunity to make my way in the world. I had discovered something far more valuable than anything I could have ever imagined. I discovered the freedom of behavior. I discovered that my personal power was built on my ability to shift another person's thoughts, feelings or both.

I learned that I should not pre-judge lessons, concepts and new information. I had the ability to change my learned behavioral habits in order to change the outcome of a situation.

I learned that it wasn't the other person's behavior that mattered. It was my own. If I wanted to change the behavior of another person then I must learn to change my own behavior first.

This lesson alone would prove to be the hallmark of

my continued success, not only in sales but also in building my organization, which later grew to over a thousand sales people proudly pitching in eleven countries around the world.

Chapter 22 Learning Points:

LIFE and BUSINESS WISDOM

Life will consistently present you opportunities to grow and learn. You must always choose to face them and deal with them if you want to stay on your path to success.

If you want to change someone's behavior you must first change your own.

EPILOGUE

I sincerely hope this book has served you. I wrote it in order to teach and inspire. It's my personal story and these are my personal experiences. It has been a pleasure writing this and reliving my experiences through these pages. I feel so grateful to my colleagues, managers, and trainers who contributed to my learning and success in the sales industry.

I have so many wonderful memories of those early days, working hard, playing hard and dreaming about our futures.

So many of the people whose names I mentioned went on to hit their goals. Many are still running their own organizations or have taken the skills they've learned and applied them to other businesses. Many have already retired because they've hit their financial goals and are simply enjoying their freedom.

As for me, I'm still chasing my dreams while exploring new places to live and thrive. In 2012, I moved my family from The Netherlands where we lived for the last twelve years to Vancouver, Canada. My wife Christina and I love the experience of living in different countries. We've set our sights on living the great life this city has to offer. I guess we needed to be surrounded by some beautiful mountains after living so long in the flatlands of Holland. My three boys have taken to the great outdoors and have fallen in love with the fantastic winter sports especially snow boarding and skiing.

Career wise I've afforded myself the privileged to take some time out to write this book and make video recordings of my highest value sales training concepts available at http://www.SalesSuccessAcademy.com. I feel blessed to have been exposed to brilliant business people who set an excellent example for me when I was young and just starting out in business. My trainings and teachings are designed to inspire, educate and motivate you the same way I was when I first started my sales career. My deeper message is to inspire you to work hard and follow your deepest dreams. My products and programs gives you access to all the business wisdom I've gleaned over the years. As well, this will not be the only book I write. I will continue to share my experiences then and now. Including how to open businesses in different countries, I learned so many lessons while opening up offices in Auckland, Sydney, London, Copenhagen and Amsterdam. As well, I want to share the amazing learning curve I experienced when I expanded my organization to Kenya and Uganda.

I want to end by encouraging you to begin. Please listen to that little voice inside your head and your heart that tells you something is possible. Please pay attention to your dreams about travelling or living in a new city or new country. Know for sure that everything is possible and the world is a very friendly place if you open up to it.

Don't allow your dreams to stay dreams. Let them have a chance to breath. Give them some light. Try things; experiment. And remember, in the worst-case scenario you can always return home. Your family, friends and loved ones will more often than not always be there for you. There's no shame in trying and you'll always have some great stories to tell.

My bet is that if you decide to take the route of your highest dreams then the opposite will happen. You will have the opportunity to invite your friends and family to join you on your new journey. You will be able to make their lives more exciting and unique than they could have ever imagined for themselves. If they choose not to come along with you, they can always stay home, cheer from the sidelines and feel proud that you had the resolve to go out into the world and fight to achieve your goals.

I encourage you to live your truth, honor your inner light and follow your bliss. Most important, when you decide to honor these three higher essentials you can't help but...

Be Bold!

Be Brave!

Be strong!

And Go for it, Today!

The world awaits your massive presence.

Sincerely yours,
Dominic Kotarski

Now that our entrepreneurial minds and spirits have connected let's keep the business conversation flowing. You can connect with me on my blog at www.DomincKotarski.com

For Next Level Sales Training video's and tools visit me at www.SalesSuccessAcademy.com

Let's get social at:
facebook.com/DominicKotarski
twitter.com/dominickotarski
ca.Linkedin.com/in/DominicKotarski
plus.google.com/+DominicKotarski

Sales Success Academy
Where Sales Success is Born

If you have enjoyed this book or found it beneficial, please do the author a favour and post a review on Amazon.com, Amazon.ca or wherever you purchased this book.

Made in the USA
Charleston, SC
28 February 2014